China's Futures

James Ogilvy and Peter Schwartz
with Joe Flower

China's Futures

Scenarios for the World's Fastest Growing Economy, Ecology, and Society

Jossey-Bass Publishers
San Francisco

Jossey-Bass books and products are available through most bookstores. To contact Jossey-Bass directly, call (888) 378-2537, fax to (800) 605-2665, or visit our website at www.josseybass.com.

Substantial discounts on bulk quantities of Jossey-Bass books are available to corporations, professional associations, and other organizations. For details and discount information, contact the special sales department at Jossey-Bass.

Manufactured in the United States of America on Lyons Falls Turin Book. This paper is acid-free and 100 percent totally chlorine-free.

Library of Congress Cataloging-in-Publication Data

Ogilvy, James A.
   China's futures: scenarios for the world's fastest growing economy, ecology, and society / by James Ogilvy and Peter Schwartz, with Joe Flower.
      p.   cm.
   Includes index.
   ISBN 0-7879-5200-1
   1. China—Social conditions—1976-   2. China—Economic conditions—1976-
   I. Title.   II. Schwartz, Peter, 1946-   III. Flower, Joe.
HN733.5.O38 2000
306'.0951 21—dc21   99-042999

FIRST EDITION
HB Printing   10 9 8 7 6 5 4 3 2

The Jossey-Bass
Business & Management Series

Contents

Preface

We offer this book neither as futurists nor as experts on China, but as practitioners of the art of scenario planning. We cannot predict the future. No one can. Nor can we know enough about China to chart its direction with certainty. But in the face of these two vast imponderables, *China* and *the future*, we can apply the art and science of scenario planning to grapple with their combined and compounded uncertainties in a methodical and useful way.

We have spent more than twenty years creating scenarios for some of the world's largest organizations, from Royal Dutch/Shell, AT&T, IBM, and Motorola to Monsanto, ARCO, Xerox, and the CIA, with dozens of others in between. When working with these giants, giant countries and their giant markets are unavoidable objects of study. As its doors to the rest of the world open wide, China looms large on the radar of global companies.

And China looms large in our imaginations as thoughtful citizens. Our children will inhabit what some forecast as the Asian century. If the nineteenth century was Europe's, and the twentieth was America's, then it is entirely possible that the twenty-first century will feature the reemergence of China as the globe's largest economy. Boasting one of the world's oldest civilizations, China has a history of opening to the world and then closing in upon its own vastness. Almost never expansionist but always influential, China just now seems to be in an opening phase of her historic rhythm.

The morning sun of history is opening the petals of this millennial morning glory . . . or oriental lotus blossom.

This book contains three very different scenarios reaching twenty years into China's future—not long, compared to China's thousands of years of history, but long enough to allow for very divergent paths. And short enough to make a major difference in our lifetimes. The content of these scenarios comes from a range of different studies conducted for large organizations that have been our clients, and the research we conducted on their behalf. There is, of course, no research today that bears a copyright of 2010. "Research" that is relevant to the future—what we call *presearch*—is a subtle blend of trend analysis and well-tutored imagination. The crafting of alternative scenarios is both a science and an art. It is based on research on the past and the present combined with a sense of history and an imagination for what is possible in the future.

When we create a set of scenarios on any given country or company or industry, we are well aware that we cannot explore all possible futures. Nor can we predict the future that will actually unfold. Forecasts are notoriously unreliable in a world as complex as ours. So our choice of scenarios is based on years of experience at choosing the most important variables around which to weave our tales.

Part One of this book contains brief treatments of some basics— the predetermined elements that will remain under all scenarios— as well as the main variables whose varying values will differentiate one scenario from another, what we call the *driving forces* of our scenarios. Part Two contains the scenarios themselves, each a linear narrative that is written like a history from a perspective more than two decades from now. Part Three draws some implications from the set of scenarios taken as a whole, as well as some suggestions on how to use these scenarios in making your own plans with respect to China's futures.

J.O. and P.S.
November 1999

Acknowledgments

While helping our clients frame their plans for dealing with China, we have joined the ranks of China watchers over the past decades. We claim no special access to the inner workings of Chinese culture or civilization. Neither of us reads or speaks Mandarin Chinese. But we have had the benefit of working with lifelong sinologists, experts who have helped us ply our trade as scenario planners. We have run workshops and projects on the future of China for a range of interested organizations that have invested billions of dollars based on the outcomes of our studies. Our main contribution was as maestros of the method—scenario planning. Others contributed more in the way of content expertise, and for that we want to thank them.

They include Orville Shell, author of numerous books on China, and his wife, filmmaker Liu Baifang; Robert Oxnam of the Asia Foundation and the Bessemer Trust; Michel Ocksenberg of the East-West Center; Michael Pillsbury from the U.S. Defense Department; Julie McCarthy of National Public Radio; Bob Broadfoot, a consultant based in Hong Kong; Ken Courtis, who represents Deutsche Bank in Tokyo; and Lucian Pye, Ken Pyle, Roger Ames, Harry Harding, Doug Paal, Robert Scalapino, John Kao, and L.Z. Yuan.

Closer to home we want to thank those who have helped us in the more immediate preparation of this book. Chris Ertel, the resident demographer at our company, Global Business Network, prepared most of the tables in this book, together with research assistance from Miles Becker and Ernesto Rodriguez. We would also like to thank Eric Best, Lawrence Wilkinson, Stewart Brand, Napier Collyns, Steve Weber, Jim Butcher, Jenny Beery, Paula Stevens, Shoshona Rosenfeld, Ben Fuller, Mollie Hazen, Lynn Carruthers, Nancy Murphy, Tina Estes, and Jennifer Kaufer for their assistance on our several China projects and in moving this book toward completion.

Our special thanks go to Oliver Freeman of Prospect Publishing in Australia and Colin Mackerras of Griffith University, Queensland, Australia, for their support in bringing our manuscript into the light of day through publication in Australia, as well as bringing it to the attention of Jossey-Bass in the United States. Among those at Jossey-Bass, we would like to thank Cedric Crocker, our editor, as well as our copy editor from Interactive Composition Corporation, Kerry Conroy.

Save for this Preface and the concluding section on how to use these scenarios, the rest of the text has passed through the fine mind and skillful hands of our professional writer, Joe Flower. Joe read through piles of our less finely tuned corporate reports and listened to whole days of conversation with us before rendering prose more readable than our own, and for this we thank him. Finally we would like to thank our wives, Tricia Ogilvy and Cathleen Schwartz, and our children, Benjamin, David, Jonathan, and Wiley, for the weekends, nights, and days of travel that might have been spent closer to home and hearth. But it is, finally, for our wives and children, and their children's children, that we feel this book is important. China's futures loom large in all of our futures.

Peter Schwartz and **James Ogilvy** are co-founders of Global Business Network in Emeryville, California. **Joe Flower** is a professional writer in San Francisco.

China's Futures

Introduction

China in the 21st Century:
The World's Biggest Story

Why China? It's the world's biggest story.

Whatever we end up calling the explosive and tortured century just ending, future historians may well see the coming century as the time of the waking of China, and they may count the millennia of Chinese civilization that came before as nothing but a giant's dreams.

The most common name on earth is not Smith or Schmidt or Valdez or Mohammed, but Li. One-fifth of all the people on the planet live in China. These 1.2 billion people are hard-working, their country is rich in resources, and they are finally free of ideology, warlords, feudalism, and nearly every other restraint that has historically held them back. According to the World Bank, over 170 million people have risen out of poverty in China in the last twenty years, more than anywhere, in any period, in the history of the world. Like a once-bewitched dragon, China is stirring from a long nightmare-riddled sleep, a staggering series of social, military, and political catastrophes that have kept it quiescent for centuries.

By various estimates of buying power (PPP, or purchasing power parity), China is already the second- or third-largest economy in the world, even while the average Chinese nominally earns a mere US$530 per year, on a par with citizens of Eritrea or Zimbabwe—and one-eighth of what the average citizen of Mexico earns. Many economists feel that number could easily grow by two, three, five times, or even more over the next twenty years. Indeed, it has already grown by six times in the past twenty years.

The success or failure of this fifth of humanity will affect everyone on the globe in ways that are hard to grasp and impossible to fully calculate. If they succeed—if in ten years, for instance, every Chinese household owns a refrigerator, a motorbike, a television, and a microwave oven—their success alone may drive up food and energy prices around the world, while it dooms all other efforts to halt global warming and protect the ozone layer.

If they fail, a China armed with nuclear and biological weapons imploding in civil war could prove the greatest human disaster the world has ever seen.

War planners picture a resurgent China battling India over influence in South Asia, battling Japan over trade and the wreckage of history, Vietnam and Indonesia over oil and trade in the South China Sea, Russia over big chunks of Siberia, Mongolia, and the Russian Far East that it took when China was weak—and battling everybody at once when it begins to feel cornered and underestimated. Optimists picture this least-aggressive of all great nations leading Asia into a long, productive "Pax Sinica" as the engine of a New Asia.

Still others picture a destabilized China breaking into four or five pieces under centrifugal, ethnic, and regional forces.

Few, if any, serious China scholars expect this vast, burdened people to stay the way they are. Their sense of themselves, of what it means to be Chinese, is already in freefall. The only question is what it will look like when its tumble is done. As this greatest opera in history plays out, Western eyes are blinded and our ears deafened by our assumptions, our ignorance, and our arrogance.

We must understand China better. We must be ready for its future, not by analyzing so carefully that we can be certain of it, but by widening our scope and deepening our feel until we can absorb its surprises. A look at China's history tells us that it never ceases to surprise—yet it never ceases to be China.

We must be responsive to China's different possible futures because a part of every history is voluntary. Vast as China is, pushed and pulled by great forces both obvious and hidden, still what we do matters. Whoever we are—Chinese, offshore Chinese, American legislators, entrepreneurs eager to get into the China market, military planners, ordinary consumers around the world—how we think of China and the decisions we make about it have an effect. Some of the brightest possibilities of China's future depend on our cooperation and involvement—and so do some of the darkest possibilities. If we will choose wisely, we have to think about China's future.

How?

But how can we think about the future? We have no crystal ball, no time machine. By its nature, the future is opaque. Yet we must think about it.

The usual method for thinking about the future looks like this: An expert armed with a great deal of information plots trends into the future (gross domestic product is rising, for example, the level of debt is staying steady, but the trees are dying), and he or she makes a guess as to which trend will stay the course and which will reverse, which will dominate and which will fade. Out of that, the expert decides on a future story, then paints that story as vividly as possible for academic, professional, and public audiences alike. The expert then defends the story, elaborates on it, and gives advice based on it.

If this method worked, we could tell by two distinct signs: 1) the smarter and more well-informed the experts are, the more their future stories converge toward a consensus, and 2) the consensus, more often than not, turns out to be correct. Simple observation shows something quite different: On China, as on almost every conceivable subject under the sun, highly informed, smart people disagree vividly and in detail. And as history unfolds, China tends to confound even the most astute and clever predictors.

The alternative is the method of the story-tellers, the tale-spinners—or, in our culture, the writers of so-called "science fiction" tales that often are not so much about science as they are about the future. World-creators like Isaac Asimov, Arthur C. Clarke, Neal Stephenson, and George Orwell succeed in helping us think about the future—and about the present that is a prelude. They did this not by trend analysis and multivariable feedback loop equations, but by weaving future tapestries rich with detail and texture—what writer John Gardner called the "vivid and continuous dream"—that allow us to see some of the future possibilities imbedded in the present (think of Orwell's *1984* or Stephenson's *Diamond Age*). We are persuaded to try on those possibilities, feel their chill, thrill to their terrors, marvel at their wonders, and find their true human size.

Our method blends the experts' analyses with the complex webs of the storytellers. We spin scenarios. We tell tales about the future, multiple tales, not as a way of hedging our bets, or taking a vote on which future has the highest probability, but as a way of thinking about the future. We do not pretend that any of our scenarios will be the correct one, a map of what actually unfolds. Rather, we hope that the scenarios represent coherent sets of possibilities that lie imbedded in the present. If you spin scenarios honestly, with good information, and with the greatest openness, you will be unlikely to get caught flat-footed. Whatever happens, you will have seen some reflection of it in your tales.

The method is not for the faint-hearted. It lacks the seeming sureness of numbers offered by econometric models and diffusion indices. Yet over the last twenty years, many of the largest companies and government agencies in the world have invited us in to spin scenarios about their futures. This book, in fact, arises out of a series of studies done for different clients—major corporations and branches of the U.S. government—consumed by the same question: How can we think about the future of China? What can we do there that makes sense? It is the very magnitude of the uncertainties in China's future that has driven them to use the scenario method.

Think about these questions as we detail the driving forces affecting China. Examine our assumptions. Listen to our future stories and ask yourself: Does this make sense? Could it happen this way?

What do you think?

Part One

The Way of China
The Magic of Context

To think about China, we have to put on the lenses of China. American, British, Japanese, Canadian, Australian—whatever our ancestry and upbringing, all of us bring with us great loads of culture, history, language, assumptions, beliefs, and traditions that blind us or distort what we see. Thinking about China, Westerners in particular see through lenses distorted by ideas about communism, Christianity, and even by our deep convictions about democracy, human rights, and the value of the individual. "We hold these truths to be self-evident." And universal. And maybe they are. But to see China, to hear it, to get some feel for it, we have to struggle to set our assumptions and beliefs aside for awhile and look through Chinese eyes. China is not Kansas or California or New South Wales, and it never will be.

1

China Basics

This is an enormous subject. Each of these basic notions has been the subject of entire books. Out of necessity, we must be terribly brief and simplistic—yet we cannot talk about the future of China without laying out some basics.

Size

China is big. This may seem too obvious to discuss, yet the sheer scale of China changes things in ways that are sometimes hard to comprehend. China is nearly as big as Russia or Canada, as wide as the United States from San Francisco to New York, and stretches north to south from fifty-four degrees to eighteen degrees north latitude. If you set it on top of North America it would fit roughly in a triangle between California's Cape Mendocino, Newfoundland in Canada's Atlantic provinces, and Haiti in the Caribbean. Set on top of Europe, the same triangle would stretch from Lisbon in Portugal, all the way across to Kazan, 400 miles east of Moscow, then south to the Red Sea, 200 miles south of Mecca.

In 1995, nearly 1.2 billion people lived in this huge land. How many people is that? Take the United States. Add on Mexico and Canada. Throw in all of Western Europe. Add Russia and Brazil. Then for good measure bring in Japan. Those twenty-two countries have roughly as many citizens as China alone. Yet the western two-thirds of China are mostly vast tracts of mountain and desert, thinly populated. The great majority of the population lives in the eastern one-third of the country. There are thirty-nine cities of more than one million people in China. Despite that amazing density, China remains the most rural of the great nations. Of those 1.2 billion people, 900 million live in villages in the countryside. China is big and getting bigger. The World Bank's best estimate is that these 1.2 billion people will become more than 1.4 billion by 2010, and nearly 1.6 billion by 2025.

China is not just another country. Thinking about China is not like thinking about France or Sudan or Brazil. It is like thinking about an entire continent, or even a planet.

China has been so big for so long, and so shut off behind mountains, desert, and ocean, that it has effectively ignored the outside world for much of its history. Its traditional name for itself is "The Middle Kingdom" or, more poetically, "All Under Heaven." Until the end of the Qing Dynasty in 1911, foreign ambassadors were dealt with through the Barbarian Office, the same office set up to deal with the border tribes such as the Mongols and the Tajiks. Imagine the German Ambassador to the United States being asked to present his credentials at the Bureau of Indian Affairs.

History

China has a lot of it. The first known emperor in China came before Moses or Homer. No other modern nation can trace its own continuous history so far back, more than 3,500 years. China started in the "elbow" of the Yangtze, west of Beijing, and spread in a series of convulsions, invasions, and migrations over the area it now occupies. For roughly half of that time, China has been united under a single emperor. Other times it has been divided into two, three, or more warring states.

Cycles

This long history moves in cycles that are so clear and have persisted for so long that some Western scholars took them as the basis for an entire theory of history—yet there is much about them that is distinctly Chinese. The *dynastic cycle* has been recognized for millennia: Revolt breaks out against a tottering old dynasty. Out of the chaos, one victor emerges, brutal and fierce, uniting the country and slaying his rivals. He becomes emperor and founds a dynasty. For several generations, things go well. The country enjoys a "golden age." Often a son or grandson, the second or third emperor in the dynasty, expands the empire, pushing back the barbarians. But eventually things start to stagnate, then to rot. Things fall apart. Taxes get heavier, the rulers wallow in hedonism, power falls into the hands of palace eunuchs and petty bureaucrats who enrich themselves and their friends. Meanwhile, brigands abound, no one tends the walls and levees—even nature seems to conspire, throwing in earthquakes, floods, and droughts. The people starve. Eventually revolts break out again, and the cycle repeats itself.

It has happened a dozen times in Chinese history. Yet even the dynastic cycle is just one example of a larger cycle between control and chaos, between a centralized government and a fragmented nation, between a fascist statism and laissez-faire times when the emperor seems far away.

Philosophically, China has veered between Confucianism, which emphasizes hierarchy, proper relationships, and ritual (and the more extreme legalism, a variety of fascism that declared the law and the state to be all and the individual nothing) and, on the other hand, Taoism, which takes government far more lightly. Laozi (nineteenth-century B.C.), the primordial Taoist, declared that governing, ideally, was as light-handed as frying a small fish.

In similar cycles, power has swung between the center and the provinces; between the rigid, hierarchical north and the experimental, entrepreneurial southeast coast; between feudal power (of which Maoism turned out to be just a special case) and capitalism; and between periods of looking inward, cutting off all contact with the outside world, and periods looking outward, trading with neighbors, and even exploring. In the fifteenth century, when Portuguese explorers first rounded the tip of Africa into the Indian Ocean, they encountered Chinese junks—in Africa. Yet for centuries afterward, China ignored the outside world, forbade contact with it, and even executed all those who returned from it. To build a ship with more than two masts was a crime punishable by death. China had turned inward again.

The twentieth century, the Republican period, from the fall of the last Qing emperor in 1911 to Mao's victory in 1949, was a period of chaos—and of reaching outward. Neither Sun Yat-sen nor Chiang Kai-shek was ever able effectively to unify the country against local warlords, the Communists, or other insurrections. The Japanese conquered the populous eastern third of the country, and the government retreated inland, relying on British and American support. The Maoist period (1949–1978) pulled the country forcibly back under central control and away from relations with the "foreign devils." Deng Xiaoping began a great relaxation of that control in 1979, but it has been so far spotty, sporadic, and confusing. From some angles, in the hiatus after Deng's death, China seems to be disintegrating, coming apart into a lawless Wild East, a lightspeed Industrial Revolution barrelling across China under the spurs of robber barons, tossing off bribes, Dickensian factories, pollution, and fortunes in gold as they go. From other angles, it looks like it has always looked—repressive, hideously petty and vindictive, only now the police, the army, and the Public Security Bureau have more money than they could ever have dreamed.

Family and Place

Every human society is a dance between the individual and the society. "No man is an island," yet each of us has our beaches and boundaries. Much of the flavor of each society comes from the emphasis: What importance do we give to the individual? What do we give to the family? To the community?

In the West, we give the greatest importance to the individual. Our movies are about individuals struggling against the odds (and often against society). Our music shows the same bent, as does our literature, our artistic traditions, and our political ideals. We talk about "rights," and picture the alternative to this individualism as fascism—absolutist government.

China has a completely different discussion going on. Except among Western-influenced intellectual elites, there is no discussion about the individual or personal rights. There are no words in Mandarin and other Chinese languages to talk about "privacy," "individualism," or "personal things," or to say, "I'm doing this for me," without the connotation of self-indulgence, selfishness, and cruel insensitivity to others. Chinese life is about the collective. The engine of the Chinese economy has been the family farm, the family business, and the village enterprise. In the traditional Chinese extended family, the family is an economic entity. Everyone who has a job or a business gives what they make to the head of the family and receives money for necessities in return. The success of the family is the success of everyone in it. All life decisions—who to marry, where to live, how to make a living—follow much the same pattern.

In the West, ever since Aristotle's philosophy of self-sufficient substances, "to be" is to be as an individual. In China, to be human is to be an appendage of a larger humanity. The difference is as deep as the grammatical divide between subject and predicate, as fundamental as geometry. In the West, a line is the shortest distance between two primary points. In the East, a point is the intersection between two lines of relationships—and it is these lines of relationship that are primary.

This sense of family is closely tied to a sense of place. While the average American moves more than once in a lifetime, the average Chinese not only never moves, but rarely travels. Many of the soldiers who fired on the students at Tiananmen Square in 1989 had never seen a university student or had never been to Beijing. The Communist Party reinforced this identification with place through an "iron triangle" of residence permits (*hukou*), secret personnel files (*dangan*), and work units (*danwei*). Until very recently, one could not travel to, for example, Shanghai without a Shanghai *hukou*, and an assignment to a Shanghai *danwei*, with the appropriate references from one's *dangan*.

This difference shades every interaction the West has with China. Western businessmen feel baffled by the seemingly impenetrable webs of *guanxi* (connections) among the Chinese. Western diplomats and politicians warning Beijing party leaders about human rights violations feel they may as well be speaking in Turkish—and they are right. The way that China looks at the individual is completely different than the way the West does.

No System

In the West, we argue constantly about what legal and political system is the right one, just how the details of it should be organized, and what rights and protections we have. The assumption behind the whole discussion is that there is a system: a legal and philosophical framework, fairly clearly delineated, within which we can work.

In China, personal rule is the model; Louis XIV's *"L'état c'est moi"* dictat makes perfect sense in Mandarin. The whole discussion is not about the system, but about the legitimacy of the government, the "mandate of heaven," or *Tianming*. That mandate is judged by the physical well-being of the people. If the people have enough to eat and are not dying from invasions or natural disasters, then heaven must be happy with the rulers. If the people are suffering, for whatever reason—war, earthquakes, famine, venal officials— then heaven has withdrawn its mandate, and before long the government will fall.

When the mandate of heaven is strong, when Confucian filial piety runs deep and people have no fear greater than the fear of losing face, China has no need for a system. If the ancient values alone will not serve, there is always *guanxi*, the intricate web of connection built of family, village, friends, and language group. But when the mandate of heaven is withdrawn and values break down, then you need laws and lawyers to constrain the individual. China has laws, and it has lawyers—some 90,000 in 1993—but it is still run, as it always has been, by *renzhi*, the rule of powerful individuals, rather than *fazhi*, the rule of law.

Three revolutions in one century—Sun's, Deng's, and particularly Mao's—have swept away what legal framework the Qing Dynasty had built, along with all the old guilds, industry associations, chambers of commerce, and laborers' associations that used to throttle commerce in the old empire and the Nationalist days. The Communist Party was the only backbone the society had. Now the Communist Party's excesses, particularly the Cultural Revolution of the 1960s and the Tiananmen Square movement of 1989, have seriously eroded the party's legitimacy. Its "mandate of heaven" had long rested on the liberation of 1949, especially on land reform. Today it stands on two legs—economic progress and stability. If either leg fails, the party stumbles and falls.

At the same time, Party rule has destroyed all the more ancient structures. Wiping out the power of the extended family and the traditional village hierarchy was an explicit goal of the establishment of the communes and of the Cultural Revolution. Today even *guanxi* has changed—what once reflected deep ties of land and family is now no more than a kind of moneyless *backsheesh*, favors given in return for favors.

For Western investors, the lack of strong, unambiguous contract law and reasonably incorruptible (or at least high-priced) courts may be the largest-single barrier to entering the Chinese economy. For Westerners in general, the lack of what looks like a system may be the largest-single barrier to understanding China.

2

Driving Forces

Split the chrysalis, and you find neither caterpillar nor nascent butterfly, but an undifferentiated, featureless pulp.

To find tomorrow's butterfly we need to take more than a surface look. We need a microscope, we need DNA analysis. We need to examine the caterpillar's markings and forebears, the branches it feeds on, and the ecological niche it occupies.

Tomorrow's China lies enfolded in the dragon's egg that is today's China.

The future is chaotic, not determinate. In any system with multiple variables, in which the results of one complex interaction become input for the next, the future state of the system is unpredictable in its very essence. China is a complex adaptive system with billions of variables. We cannot know its future.

But we can analyze its present, searching for the deep drivers that are most likely to shape its future. And out of those deep driving forces, we can shape scenarios, ways of thinking about China's possible futures.

We have identified, and will describe in more detail in the following pages, fourteen broad driving forces that will help shape whatever future China grows into:

The Mighty Renminbi: Money is the mother of all change in today's China.

Too Much Government and Not Enough: This represents the continued devolution of China's internal politics.

Cultural Freefall: In the land of VCRs, lipstick, and Lexuses, what's a Chinese to believe in?

The Huaqiao, *or Offshore Chinese:*   They form a diaspora more ancient and far more influential than that of any other country.

Centrifugal Forces: These forces are reducing the power of Beijing over provinces and regions.

Demographics: China's population—its sheer size, its composition, and its distribution—is unique in history in several ways.

Black Air, Gray Water: Degradation of the environment may prove a crucial stumbling block.

Chips and Fiber: Technology is enabling many of the swift changes sweeping through China.

The People's Liberation Army: This organization forms the single largest economic organization in China.

The Communist Party: It was the engine of China's swift transformation fifty years ago, now fading.

The "Class of '77":   This term represents the group of younger leaders poised to take control in Beijing.

The Flea and the Elephant: Hong Kong is the flea in a race to transform China before China transforms it.

Who's the Bully?:   China's relations with its neighbors and the world.

The United States: It is the world's largest economic and military force, which has long thought of itself as having a special relationship with China.

The Mighty *Renminbi*

In 1978, and more intensely in his 1992 tour of Southern China, Deng Xiaoping changed China's economic model. In the Great Leap Forward and the Cultural Revolution, Mao had held up to the country a specific, and quite singular, model of low-level industrial and agricultural activity widely distributed in communes that were larger than villages but far smaller than the massive aggregations of capital and assets characteristic of Western economies. It was a political model, designed specifically to show that you can create common wealth without creating plutocrats, wealthy people with power over others' lives.

It failed spectacularly.

It not only failed to improve the lot of most of China's people, but it took away much of what the peasants had gained from the land reform of the early 1950s. It created a new class of plutocrats—the party elite themselves. The new and explicit model that rose out of Deng's vague pronouncements in favor of profit and pragmatism was the polar opposite of Mao's. It called for large-scale economic integration and the intensive use of capital to put more people to work more productively.

So far, it has worked spectacularly. It has raised more people out of absolute poverty and starvation faster than anything else ever done in the history of the world. If results were all, if you could do moral calculus on an abacus, if lives saved cancelled lives destroyed, then Deng Xiaoping would be worth ten Gandhis or 100 Mother Teresas. In the six years between 1979 and 1985, in the countryside alone, an estimated 150 to 170 million people were lifted from the edge of starvation to making a reasonable living, as a direct result of the reforms Deng pushed through at the third plenary session of the Eleventh Central Committee of the Communist Party of China in December 1978. The percentage of children who die in their first year has dropped from 5.6 to 3.8—which means that the extra income is saving 378,000 children's lives every year.

Since 1978, China's economy has grown at a rate that few fore-casters would have believed, averaging 8–9 percent real growth all through the 1980s, and leaping as high as 13 percent in 1993. In the middle of 1998, the government announced its disappointment that the economy had grown at only 7 percent in the first half of the year—that, at a time when several major Asian economies were recording negative growth. Such rapid growth in so large a nation dwarfs even the rise of the "miracle" economies of Japan and Germany since World War II. Even after adjusting for inflation, average Chinese are making over three times what they were when Deng let slip the dogs of capitalism.

The effect of this astonishing growth is hard to measure exactly— the relationship between China's financial statistics and reality is endlessly debatable—but the clear existence of this growth and its astonishing magnitude resound all through the numbers. For instance, the number of connected telephone lines rose from a mere 4 million in 1980 (one for every 250 people) to 57 million in 1995 (one for every twenty-one people), and was growing at 35 percent per year. The average Chinese had two-and-a-half times as much liv-ing space in 1995 as in 1978. Adjusted for inflation, consumption was 3.5 times higher. In 1978, the authorities had not bothered ask-ing how many people had televisions. In 1980, only four houses in a thousand had them, but by 1995, according to official statistics, 90 percent of all urban Chinese households owned a color television set.

Fuel

The fuel of this amazing growth has been overseas investment and high savings. Foreign investment, negligible and essentially illegal in the Maoist years, climbed to nearly US$10 billion per year by 1985, and passed US$100 billion in 1995, growing all through the early 1990s at a rate of more than 50 percent per year—each year half again more than the year before.

Adjusted for inflation, personal savings deposits were forty times larger in 1995 than 1978, reaching nearly 3 trillion yuan (over

US$350 billion). That rise might seem hardly credible except for the fact that Chinese everywhere else put very high proportions of their personal income in the bank, a reasonable response to a history that includes wars, expulsions, famines, and political convulsions of unimaginable scale. In an article in the *Harvard Business Review* called "The Worldwide Web of Chinese Business" about the "life-raft" values of the typical Chinese entrepreneur, John Kao (a professor at Harvard Business School) included: "A high, even irrational level of savings is desirable, regardless of immediate need" (pp. 24–36). In China, after 1978, people were finally making enough money to put some away, and for the first time since the Maoist revolution they had a choice of banks to put them in—banks that competed by raising their interest rates high enough above the levels of inflation to attract depositors.

This enormous amount of personal savings gives the Chinese economy not only fuel for more growth, but a certain cushion against big mistakes—as long as hyperinflation does not wipe it out.

Poverty

Still, the access to this better life has been wildly uneven. At the same time that the average Chinese is doing much better, the poorest of the poor are not keeping up. According to a 1996 World Bank report, in 1978 nearly 60 percent of all Chinese lived on the equivalent of a dollar a day or less. By 1987, that had fallen to 30 percent. Beijing has been spending roughly US$1 billion per year trying to eliminate rural poverty, but a 1996 government report showed that $800 million of that is given in subsidies to rural counties—and apparently, that is where most of the money stops, in the county seats. Little, if any, finds its way out to the peasants. Many peasants complain, in fact, that they have never seen anybody from the county, even though their village may be only a few miles from the county seat.

In September 1996, Lin Junwen, a senior staff member of Premier Li Peng's working group on poverty, spoke to reporters with surprising frankness. He admitted that to reach the goal of abolishing the most extreme poverty in China by the year 2000, "That means that we must lift 13 million people out of poverty annually, almost three times the figure we have managed to reach in the last few years. . . . The poverty in which these 65 million people are living constitutes the hardest nut to crack due to the various deep-rooted geographical and socioeconomic adversities." Translation: The 350 million or more peasants who have crept out of most dire poverty in the past fifteen years were the easy ones to help—they were Chinese who lived on flat, well-watered land, with access to transportation. The ones that are still poor are the minorities at the edge of China, in the mountains, plateaus, and deserts, with little good soil, rainfall, or transportation.

At the same time—for the first time since the Maoist revolution—an urban class of deeply poor people, perhaps as many as 15 million, is developing. They are castoff workers in a society with a threadbare safety net.

Human compassion aside, having so many people mired in such deep, seemingly intractable poverty is one factor that could hold China back from fulfilling its great promise.

State-owned Firms

As late as the mid-1990s, state-owned firms (SOEs) still employed some 115 million workers (70 percent of the industrial workforce) and used some 75 percent of all assets, yet they generated only one-third of the country's industrial production, and a mere 1 percent of its profit. Of course, they were not designed for profit. They were designed to provide employment to as many people as possible, regardless of their efficiency, and to serve the larger society. A large *danwei*, such as a hospital or a steel plant, is similar to what we would call a classic "company town"—they provide their employees not only wages but, typically, housing, education, medical care, and even recreation. To serve the larger society, these enterprises are often ordered by Beijing to sell their product—particularly energy products such as oil and coal—at less than they cost to produce.

These state-owned enterprises have already begun to change, but slowly, haltingly, in a start-and-stop, two-steps-forward-one-back rhythm that plays to the beat of economic cycles and political interests. Beijing enacted a basic bankruptcy law in 1986 (though not much has been done with it). Unemployment insurance, retirement funds, and job-retraining programs are growing in some provinces and cities. In this decade, many of the state-owned firms have been "corporatized"—given boards that are separate from the bureaucracies that own them. Others have been turned into joint ventures with foreign firms. Many have been allowed to keep their profits in return for taking on responsibility for their costs, and have been exposed to direct competition from foreign companies, TVEs (Town and Village Enterprises), and other government agencies, such as the People's Liberation Army (PLA). Such firms often link bonuses to increased profit. Many have even farmed out their management to the highest bidder—whoever writes a business plan that credibly promises the highest return to the state gets to run the company.

In September 1997, the Fifteenth Communist Party Congress announced its determination to corporatize the state-owned enterprises. At the same time, the government announced measures to try and find jobs for those millions of people who would be thrown out of work by this measure.

The privatization of the state-owned enterprises will go a long way towards relaxing their grip on the economy. It shows a great deal of courage on the part of the post-Deng leadership that they are so determined to go down that track, especially since they have made the decision just at the time when most other countries of the region are suffering serious financial and economic crisis. The likelihood is that the enormous losses that the state-owned enterprises sustained in the past, estimated at fully 3 percent of the gross domestic product (GDP) in 1992, will be minimized or even cancelled out in the future.

Yet there are two points to remember that must counter the expectation of a much more competitive economy. The first is that among the 100,000 or so state-owned enterprises, less than 1,000 take up a significant proportion of the total size. The likelihood is there will not be many privatizing inroads into these large state-owned enterprises. The second point is that, for all its ameliorating measures, the government is already faced with a serious unemployment problem, people who have spent their lives thinking that the state would protect them from unemployment, only to find themselves cast on the scrapheap. These people are a potential source of social unrest. Many have already found alternative employment, but there are quite a few who are finding the going very tough indeed.

Inflation

Another symptom in China's febrile economy is inflation. The institutions that other countries use to control inflation—especially a strong, politically independent central banking system—are weak or nonexistent in China. The country's central bank, the People's Bank of China (until the 1980s, the country's only bank), is still, like most other institutions, controlled by the Party. On the other hand, it has loose and weakening control over other banks, and even over its own provincial and municipal divisions.

Under control until 1987, inflation suddenly jumped to 18 percent in 1988–89. The government's ferocious response to the inflation crashed the economy in 1989 and 1990, when growth slowed to 4 percent. When the economy roared back in the early 1990s, inflation roared back with it, peaking at 22 percent in 1994. Each time inflation has reared its ugly head, Beijing has knocked it down, but each time it has raised its head higher. In 1993, Zhu Rongji was appointed senior vice-premier with responsibility for the economy, and in 1998 he succeeded the unpopular Li Peng as premier. He took vigorous action to control inflation and had brought it down to near zero by the middle of 1998.

Yet the fact remains that inflation is an ever-present danger in China. A financial crisis (much like the one that Mexico has gone through in this decade), with inflation spiraling out of control, wiping out the savings of hundreds of millions of people, wrecking the economy, bringing on severe depression and chaotic political and military reactions, is an all-too-real possibility for China. Whether Beijing will continue to have the power to keep inflation under control is a big question in China's future.

Other flash points include:

- *Cycles*. Rapidly growing economies, like Japan's in the 1960s, like the U.S. economy in the late 1800s, are prone to wild expansions and contractions. China has undergone four distinct cycles since 1978. These boom-and-bust cycles in other countries have led to migrations, labor unrest, and at times, revolution.

- *Unemployment*. Maoist censuses had no line for unemployment—the concept officially did not exist. The 1982 census listed 145 million unemployed. By 1990, that had risen to 170 million. By the mid-1990s, an estimated 50–100 million workers—the "floating population"—camped out near railway stations, set up squatter towns near Beijing and Shanghai, and flooded into the coastal region seeking work. The privatization of the state-owned enterprises can only make the unemployment problem worse.

- *Barriers to trade*. Access to China's potentially enormous market can be challenging for outsiders. The barriers include tariffs and an array of cultural obstacles, along with the lack of such things as real, enforceable intel-lectual property laws, independent, incorruptible courts, a clear body of contract law, access to critical trade information, and a transparent, nonarbitrary set of commercial regulations. At the same time, other major traders (especially the United States) have thrown up roadblocks to China's joining the World

Trade Organization, the General Agreement on Tariffs and Trade, and other multinational trade structures.

- *Energy access.* If China succeeds at all, it will need enormous amounts of energy. As of 1991, for instance, China consumed the equivalent of 602 kilograms of oil for each citizen, while the United States consumed 7,681 kilograms per capita. Any modernization of China translates directly into a massive energy problem—and not just for China.

  China's own energy reserves are problematic. It has plenty of coal (900 years' worth at current consumption rates), but it is dirty, high-sulfur coal. Much has been made of new oil discoveries, but one oil industry expert referred to it as "poor-quality oil, full of heavy metals, hard to refine. In fact, it will cost about 25 percent more to refine it—and the work is technologically difficult. Only a few Western oil companies have the technology to handle it."

Much has also been made about the reserves in the far-west Tarim Basin and in the South China Sea, especially in the area of the hotly contested Spratly Islands (and the aptly named "Mischief Reef"), but these reserves are, in fact, modest compared to China's emerging energy needs.

So China is not going to get rich on oil, and by some estimates it had already turned from a net exporter of oil to an importer in 1993.

One big issue is: Will China be able to bring natural gas from the huge reserves of Siberia?

But the larger issue is the disconcerting image of a rapidly growing, increasingly well-armed and assertive China forced to look beyond its borders for the energy to feed its huge industrial fires. Pessimists point out that what led Japan to attack Pearl Harbor just half a century ago was an industrial and military thirst for the oil of Southeast Asia and Indonesia.

Too Much Government and Not Enough

Whether most Chinese are eager for a Western-style democracy, complete with votes and a bill of rights, is not all that clear. It is clear that they want to be able to make choices over their own lives.

April Lynch, a reporter for the *San Francisco Chronicle*, watched the last demonstration in Hong Kong commemorating the June 4, 1989, Tiananmen Square Massacre—the last before the colony's reversion to Chinese rule. In the crowd around dissident Han Dongfang, Lynch talked to Wendy Mok, a mother with a six-year-old child in tow, who told her: "That is all I want for my kids after July 1. I want them to be able to hear a protester like Mr. Han if they want, or just be able to go to the movies if they'd rather do that instead. I want them to have choices. We have choices now. . . . They shouldn't disappear when July is here" ("Hong Kong Celebrating . . . ," June 2, 1997).

She could well have spoken for her neighbors already living in China. Historically, the presence of a large and solid middle class in any country has led to a demand for personal freedoms and a sense of choice. The rapid expansion of a genuine middle class in China will likely lead to the same pressures—and it already has. In contrast to the revolutionary terror of the Cultural Revolution, citizens of today's China can work more or less where they want, live more or less where they choose, and say whatever they like, as long as they refrain from publicly challenging the government. To an American, that would be a very large exception, and for some Chinese it is as well. Whether it is for most Chinese lies behind one of the big questions in China's future: Is authoritarian government, Communist or otherwise, a permanent aspect of China? Or is some form of real democracy possible?

Already, democracy is being tried at the village level. A 1987 law allows towns and villages to choose their own leaders. As of 1995, more than 80 percent of China's villages had done just that, electing some 4.2 million officials, most of them by secret ballot with universal suffrage. And only about 60 percent of those elected are members of the Communist Party.

Furthermore, though Beijing continues to impose candidates for local and provincial offices, in a number of cases since 1993, local and provincial party officials have forced Beijing to back down on its choice and accept a different candidate. Chinese citizens may even now legally sue their government—though few do. Clearly, in many ways, the monolithic nature of Beijing's rule is shifting.

In most authoritarian cultures (such as the Soviet Union), politics and economic development have not been aligned. Political power was won at the expense of the economy, and the central government saw economic power as a problem and a rival. Today's China seems to be attempting something different. In order to allow entrepreneurialism and economic freedom, it has loosened the rules of the game enough that politics rarely stand in the way of economics. The most graphic example of this is that Beijing allows state enterprises and agencies of the government, such as the People's Liberation Army, to own private enterprises, but usually it will not give them monopolies. Through their personal involvement in the marketplace and their dependence on the money they make, most government bureaucrats and party cadres strongly support the new economic freedoms. They will resist (or simply find ways around) any attempt to cut them back.

So there is the tension: On one hand, economic liberalization requires some loosening of the rules, allows people to make choices about their lives, and supports a middle class that will demand more choice and personal freedoms. On the other hand, China's authoritarian elite is deeply entrenched, and China has no real experience with Western-style democracy.

The memories of living Chinese are filled with horrors inflicted both by too much government (the regimentation of the Great Leap Forward, and the petty block-by-block and village-by-village dictatorship of local party committees and bureaucrats all through the Communist era) and by too little government (the breakdown and chaos of wartime China, the mob rule and destruction of all traditions in the Cultural Revolution, and today's rampant corruption).

Though we in the West have an image of China as the land of intrusive government, in many ways, China does not have enough government to manage such a huge population and its burgeoning economy. According to the World Bank, China spends a mere 9 percent of its gross domestic product (GDP) on government at all levels, while Taiwan and the United States both spend 16 percent of GDP; Russia spends 17 percent; Germany, 18 percent; France, 20 percent; and the United Kingdom, 22 percent. China lacks the equivalent of—or has only a pale shadow of—such U.S. agencies as the Securities and Exchange Commission, the Federal Reserve, the Environmental Protection Agency, the Federal Deposit Insurance Corporation, the Occupational Safety and Health Administration, and the Social Security Administration, among many others.

Any government or movement that promised to establish a rule of law, while allowing people a reasonable amount of personal freedoms—especially freedom from bureaucratic interference—would garner massive support among the Chinese people. But whether it will turn out that way is not at all clear.

Cultural Freefall

China is in a cultural freefall. In a single century, the world's largest nation has made three abrupt breaks with the past: the fall of the Qing, Maoism and the Cultural Revolution, and Deng's break with Mao. Mao, especially, lit the fires of the Great Leap Forward and then the Cultural Revolution explicitly to destroy all the underpinnings of the past, to "bury Confucius," and with him the family and the village. More than anything else, the Maoist years destroyed the power of the family to protect its members from the government.

To a surprising extent, Mao succeeded in destroying the old China. But he failed to create a new one. The vacuum he left is being filled by money and its symbols—lipstick and Lexuses and the art of the deal. A search for China's soul might not seem a pragmatic quest—and yet it may shape China's future as much as any other single factor.

What does it mean today to be Chinese? Is greed enough to hold a nation together? Or must there be something deeper, some vision larger than the pursuit of money and power?

Clearly many Chinese are searching. Beginning early in the 1990s, a cult of Mao swept the nation. Mao amulets appeared swinging from the rearview mirrors of buses and taxis. Mao temples and shrines sprang up. "The old guy," as people referred to him, became a good-luck charm and, of all things, a token of success. Yet it is not Mao's ideas, or Marx's, that are attracting adherents. As Nicholas Kristof put it pithily in China Wakes (1995): "There are about as many believing Communists in China as there are Zoroastrians in the West." Especially after the Tiananmen Square crackdown, this loss of faith has extended into the highest reaches of the party itself. Ideology is dead.

At the same time, especially in the south, Christianity has become the new rage, the "cool" Western thing, much as various Eastern religions took root in the West in the 1960s and 1970s. It is estimated that there are ten times as many Christians in China today as there were under Chiang Kai-shek. Alongside mainstream Christianity, semi-Christian cults reminiscent of the Taipings are spreading.

Even more popular all across China is the mass cult of qi gong. Though it is at its root a yoga-like protocol of breath control and meditation, masters of qi gong often claim extraordinary powers, such as being able to heal the sick, fly, weld metal, light things on fire with a touch, fall on the point of a sword and break it, or transport objects through the air (even through solid walls). Belief in these masters is growing rapidly, even among the sophisticated and powerful. The government in Beijing, in fact, keeps its own qi gong master named Zhang Baosheng, called "a national treasure" by a Public Security Ministry spokesman.

The party itself is searching for something for people to believe in, going so far in 1994 as to host a grand national celebration for the 2,545th birthday of Confucius—the exemplar of everything Mao tried to destroy.

The erosion of values shows up even in the sea of official statistics. Divorces, for instance, have risen nationally from 340,000 couples in 1980 (a year when more than 7 million couples married) to over 1 million couples in 1995 (when 9.3 million couples married). In recent years, the number of marriages has maintained steadily, while the divorces have steadily climbed—this in a culture in which the family is society's bedrock, and marriage is the center of the family.

At the same time, people are streaming into the cities. When Mao took over China, nearly 88 percent of the people lived in the countryside—that is to say, almost everyone. By 1980, that had dropped to 80 percent, and by 1997 to 70 percent. More and more Chinese have lost their attachment to the "good earth" and to their *laojia* (ancestral home).

Can Chinese values and culture reemerge? At our meeting in Hong Kong in February 1997, filmmaker Liu Baifang, who was raised in Beijing and fled the Cultural Revolution, asked, "When you sever the roots, what can grow?"

Yet cultural values are very hard to kill. They live in the deep structures of the society, in the ins and outs of language, in the way mothers hold their children. It is not only Christianity but traditional religions like Buddhism that are reviving. Among particular minorities, Islam and Tibetan Buddhism retain enormous social influence.

Now that the iron grip of Maoism has relaxed, China needs a center. It needs strong laws and good courts, but even more, it needs deep values. Two questions in China's future are, where will it find those values, and how strong will they be?

Huaqiao: The Offshore Chinese

For centuries, with every convulsion, China has spilled people out across the South China Sea to its neighbors, to Vietnam, Burma, Thailand, Malaysia, Singapore, Indonesia, the Philippines, and in this century and the last, to the United States. They include peasants, bankers, doctors, entrepreneurs, and others. Over time they have formed a vast web of networks reaching across the globe—and each back to their own *laojia,* the people in their small corner of China who came from the same village or the one down the road, who speak the same language in the same tones, the Hakka, the Taishan Cantonese, the Teochiu, the Hokkien, Hokchia, Hokchiu, Henghua, and Wu. Now these great networks of *huaqiao,* or "Chinese sojourners," are reaching back through the network, pouring billions of dollars back into their homelands.

By the mid-1990s, more than 60 million Chinese lived overseas, half in Taiwan (with 21 million) and Hong Kong (6 million), with another 2 million in Singapore. Commercially powerful, dominant minorities spread all through Southeast Asia. In a wired world of high-speed travel and communications, this diaspora becomes a source of strength and tremendous leverage in a global economy. The *huaqiao* represent a powerful set of organizing forces that will help to shape the future of China. They bring three things back to China:

1. *Capital* that is large-scale, mobile, and intimately connected to China

2. *Knowledge,* comprising business acumen, technical know-how, and a broad awareness of how the rest of the world works

3. A *cultural reservoir of Chinese identity* built up outside China, another model for being Chinese that brings the traditional values into the modern world

Their capital is impressive by any standards. Economists are used to speaking of the commercial world as having three poles: Europe, the

United States, and Japan. But some argue that there is a fourth pole of equal stature—a "Greater China" that lumps the Chinese economy together with those of Hong Kong, Taiwan, and Singapore. A 1993 World Bank report put the GDP of this Greater China (in purchasing power terms) at US$2.5 trillion, already more than that of Japan, and nearly half as big as that of the United States. The same report estimated that "Greater China" would surpass the United States by 2002, with a purchasing power GDP twice as big as Japan's and three times that of Germany. Combine this productivity with the high savings rate seen among Chinese everywhere, and the overseas Chinese are sitting on truly astonishing piles of cash. Tiny Taiwan, for instance, holds the world's largest foreign reserves. In his book *Asia Rising* (1995), financial analyst Jim Rohwer estimates that "towards the end of the 1990s the private cash holdings of the overseas Chinese should easily exceed $3 trillion."

And they are not ladling this capital carefully into small experiments in China; they are pouring it in. It is estimated that fully three-quarters of the hundreds of billions of dollars of investment capital flowing into China is coming from overseas Chinese. Beijing is shrewdly encouraging this flow. All of China's "special economic zones" are set up all along the southeast coast, because that is the area that more than 90 percent of overseas Chinese call home.

At the upper levels of personal wealth, the overseas Chinese are a particularly peripatetic bunch, winging between homes in Hong Kong, Vancouver, London, and Singapore like pelagic seabirds. Some spend so much time in the air that they have earned the nickname "astronauts," and their children the title "parachute kids," for the way they come in from the sky for the holidays from their boarding schools.

When *huaqiao* come back to the villages and counties that they or their ancestors fled, bringing with them money and presents, wearing fine Western suits and bearing tales of globe-spanning commercial networks and enterprises that sound like magic cash machines, they instantly become role models for those who stayed behind.

Their very existence sets up a vision of a different future, of a China that is vigorous, prosperous, and unfettered by party or borders.

But the vision is not just about money. These *huaqiao* are bearers not just of the new ways, but of the old—of the dominance of family, clan, and village, the importance of face, the predominance of values. They are a root that has not been cut back.

Centrifugal Forces

Beijing seems to be losing control over China's far-flung pieces and places. Official statistics show a massive shift in government financing: in 1980, of all the revenues taken in by Chinese governments, only one-quarter went directly to the central government, yet Beijing spent over half of the money going out. In other words, the provinces and municipalities were massively shipping money to Beijing for the mandarins of the capital to spend as they saw fit.

Today it is the other way around: Though Beijing now raises more than half of all revenues in China, it only gets to spend 29 percent of them. The rest it ships to the local governments, who spend more than 70 percent.

These dry numbers mask an enormous power struggle. During the reforms of the 1980s, Beijing exported both responsibilities and revenues to the provinces. In the 1990s, it has attempted in many instances to reassert control over policy and recapture revenue streams—and it has consistently failed.

At the same time, some authorities point to massive imbalances in the rates of growth of the coast and the interior. Every province and region is growing, but some much faster than others. In 1992, for instance, the economies of the coastal provinces Jiangsu and Fujian grew by a whopping 26 percent and 20 percent, respectively, and the economy of the tiny island province of Hainan ballooned by an astonishing 40 percent, while Tibet, the far Western province Qinghai, and the far Northern province Heilongjiang expanded by only 7 percent. Other authorities argue that the fact that everyone's life is getting better is more important than the fact that some are doing better than others. They also point out that many of the people working in coastal factories are people from the interior—and they are sending home remittances that, in turn, are driving the growth of their home villages. Besides those arguments, the imbalances have flattened out somewhat: By 1995, the coastal provinces were growing at a 14–16 percent rate, and the interior at an 8–9 percent rate.

Another "centrifugal force" is the two far Western "autonomous regions," Tibet and Xinjiang and their main inhabitants, the Tibetans and Uygurs. In the 1990s, there has been a series of secessionist movements in both areas. Tibet has gained much more publicity in the West, because of the popularity of Tibetan Buddhism there, taken up in a big way in 1997 by Hollywood. But Xinjiang is actually more dangerous for the Chinese leaders, because Islam, the religion of the Uygurs, is much more ready than Tibetan Buddhism to organize violent opposition to Chinese rule and to seek military assistance from supporters over the borders. In February 1997, there were serious riots in northwestern Xinjiang, which caused considerable bloodshed. In the Xinjiang capital, Ürümqi, there were bus bombs set off by Uygur terrorists on the same day that the funeral for Deng Xiaoping was taking place in Beijing (February 25, 1997). It seemed they wanted to thumb their nose at the memory of the leader, an insult of enormous proportions.

The response of the Chinese government has been the "carrot and stick" approach. The stick means that they suppress any signs of secessionism quickly and firmly, even brutally. The carrot means that they do all they can to make it worth the while of the Tibetans, Uygurs, and other minorities to remain part of China. The main part of this carrot is to raise the living standards of the people. Great efforts have been made to improve the economic level of the Far West. An official report from 1998 had it that the Tibetan economy had posted double-digit growths each year from 1993 to 1997, being above the national average over the period.

Whether this strategy will work in the long term remains to be seen, but nobody should underestimate the importance of national unity in either China's psyche or recent history. Few would consider the actual dissolution of China a good thing—or more than a remote possibility. But some argue that a relaxation of Beijing's grip over the provinces brings a measure of flexibility to the system that it will need to survive the turbulence ahead.

Demographics

Exhibit 1. China's Population Future:
1.45 Billion by 2020—Give or Take North and South Korea

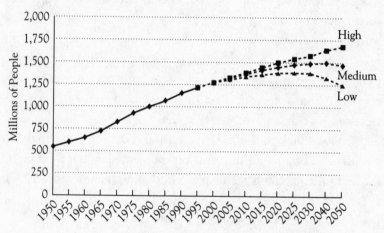

Source: United Nations, World Population Prospects: The 1998 Revision.

The period of China's most rapid population growth was 1963–1973, during which time the country grew at a rate of about 2.5 percent per year (for a doubling time of just twenty-eight years), or by nearly 20 million persons a year. It has since been slowly tapering off. During the 1990s, the growth rate leveled off to just under 1 percent a year (for a doubling time of about seventy years), almost exactly the same rate as the United States today. Total population growth in the 1990s has averaged about 10 million new people per year.

As for the future projections, the United Nations "medium" series for China calls for the population to grow to about 1.45 billion by 2020, or an increase of roughly 225 million over today's population (a growth of about 19 percent). The "high" projection weighs in at 1.51 billion, the "low" projection at 1.37 billion. The only difference between high, medium, and low estimates in the U.N. projections are the fertility rate assumptions used (of 2.43, 2.1, and 1.5, respectively, by 2020).

It is interesting to note that the projections were substantially revised between 1994 and 1996. The revisions are shown in Table 2.1. The "medium" projections for 2020 were therefore reduced by 39 million persons between 1994 and 1996 (or by 3.6 percent). The key difference between the 1994 and 1996 projections, though, was the reduction of the high-level fertility assumption from 2.5 to 2.43. As a result, the total spread between high and low projections to 2020 was substantially reduced—from 234 million to 143 million persons.

For this reason, we had to change the title to this graph from "1.5 Billion by 2020—Give or Take Japan" to "1.45 Billion by 2020—Give or Take North and South Korea." Not quite as catchy, perhaps, but this is the current reality as the United Nations sees it. Of course, the spread between high and low gets much wider the further out you go; by 2050, it ranges between 1.77 billion and 1.20 billion—or a cool 570 million.

Table 2.1. U.N. Projections for China's Population in 2020

	1994 Projections	1996 Projections	Difference	
High	1,595,682,000	1,509,389,000	−86,293,000	(−5.4%)
Medium	1,488,075,000	1,448,818,000	−39,257,000	(−2.6%)
Low	1,361,692,000	1,366,031,000	+4,339,000	(+0.3%)
Spread (Hi-Low)	233,990,000	143,358,000	−90,632,000	(−38.7%)

Finally, it is important to note that China's population is expected to continue growing throughout this period despite replacement-level fertility in the medium projections. This is due to the phenomenon known as "population momentum," in which any country that has undergone rapid fertility decline still typically experiences population growth for a generation or so due to the increasing numbers of women that enter childbearing age as a result of previous large cohorts of children. (The flattening out of the population "pyramid" takes a long time.) Only when the number of women of childbearing age starts to fall will population growth truly stabilize (unless fertility levels plunge well below the replacement level). For this reason, note that the "medium" U.N. projections, which assume replacement-level fertility of 2.1, do not result in zero population growth until 2030.

Exhibit 2. China:
The Billion-Pound Gorilla in World Population

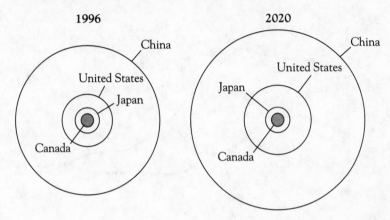

In order to show just how big China's population is (and is projected to be), we compare its total population for 1996 and 2020 to that of seven countries that Americans are used to thinking of as "important": the United States, Russia, Japan, Mexico, Germany, the United Kingdom, and Canada. In the table below, the population totals for the entire world are shown.

	1997	2020
Brazil	163,689,184	209,637,000
Canada	30,286,600	33,630,000
China	1,227,176,704	1,428,692,000
Germany	82,071,000	78,889,000
India	962,377,664	1,266,021,000
Indonesia	200,390,288	263,937,000
Japan	126,091,000	123,289,000
Mexico	94,348,864	127,545,000
Russian Federation	147,307,008	136,977,000
United Kingdom	59,009,000	59,763,000
United States	267,636,000	303,795,000
World	**5,819,554,816**	**7,444,925,000**

Source: World Bank, 1999 World Development Indicators (CD-Rom)

Exhibit 3. China's Fertility Freefall:
From Six Kids to Two in One Generation

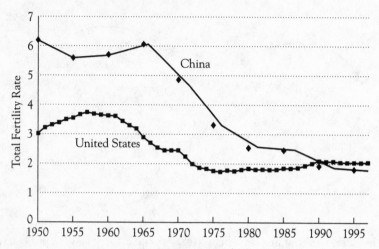

Source: United Nations, *World Population Prospects: The 1998 Revision;* U.S. Census Bureau, *Current Population Reports, U.S.*

It is truly difficult for Americans to realize just how shocking this picture is. According to writers Griffith Feeney and Wang Feng: "The decline (of fertility in China), in the largest country in the world, occurred far more rapidly than any other recorded country-level decline in history."[1] A fertility decline this steep disrupts basic social reality at so many levels, it is hard to know where to begin. Just recall for a moment the prolonged impact that the Baby Boom has had on the fertility rate in the United States—a rise from about 2.5 to 3.5 children per woman of child-bearing age, then back to 2.0 in a couple of decades. Now multiply the effect of this transition on U.S. culture, economy, and society by a factor of ten for some idea of what has happened in China. It is no less than revolutionary at every level—economic, family structure, personal conceptions of identity, and so on.

[1] Feeney G., and W. Feng, "Parity Progression and Birth Intervals in China: The Influence of Policy in Hastening Fertility Decline," *Population and Development Review*, March 1993: p. 95.

One Child

Another demographic quirk may have strange and unpredictable consequences starting about 2008. China's fierce "one-child" population control policy has resulted in a drastic drop in the country's rate of growth—indeed, the biggest fertility drop in history but at the most draconian cost. The policy is implemented at times at the village level through forced sterilizations, heavy fines, and even destroying the houses of those who break the rules. Increasingly, Chinese children are being raised as little emperors, doted on by parents and grandparents who greatly outnumber them. But another inadvertent result of the policy may have even stranger effects: As ultrasound and amniocentesis increasingly allow parents to know the sex of the fetus (in a society that values boys far more than girls), far more boys than girls have been born. There are roughly six boys for every five girls under the age of ten in China now. What does that do to the status of women and the nature of marriage when those boys grow old enough to look for wives?

At the same time, what happens to the extensive and ancient system of *guanxi* (connection)—so much of which is based on family connections through second cousins and great uncles—in a world of one-child families?

Finally, will the policy last? Or will other great driving forces loosen the grip of Beijing over people's daily lives? Will the nearly 1 billion rural Chinese go back to the six-child families of recent memories and enter an out-of-control doubling spiral of truly Malthusian proportions? If in the future, China grew at the rate that it did in the forty years from 1950 to 1990, then by the year 2070—within the life span of some babies born today—China's population would reach 5 billion people, nearly the population of the entire globe today. It would, that is, if the land would support that many people, if this explosion of people did not lead instead to a massive famine, a die-off of horrifying proportions.

Exhibit 4. One Child Policy? Fine, So Long As It's A Boy

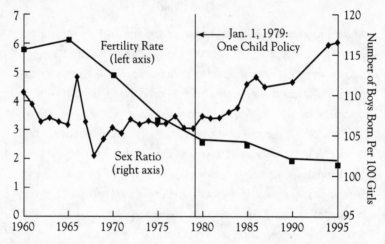

Source: Johansson and Nygren (1991); China Statistical Yearbook (various editions); United Nations, World Population Prospects: The 1996 Revision.

The main point of this graph should be quite clear: By the time the one-child policy was implemented in January 1, 1979, China's fertility rate had already fallen sharply to about 2.5. The previous policy of "later, longer, fewer" had already done the job (promoting family planning through later marriage, longer birth intervals, and fewer children). Although the one-child policy can certainly be credited with contributing to further decline, its main impact has been a radically skewed sex ratio at birth, from 106 boys born per 100 girls in 1979 to nearly 117 boys in 1995 (the biological norm is between 105 and 106 boys per 100 girls). There are four main reasons cited in the literature for the skewed sex ratios. In rough order of importance (by consensus), they are: underreporting of female births, which may account for as much as half of the sex ratio gap[2]; selective abortion, with the help of modern ultra-

[2]Johansson S. and O. Nygren, "The Missing Girls of China: A New Demographic Account," Population and Development Review, March 1991: 35–51. Underreporting of female births is of course related to the orphanage crisis in China, places that are full of unwanted (and often unreported) girls.

sound technology[3]; neglect of female babies and young children, especially in rural areas; and female infanticide (generally considered to be rare).

The skewed sex ratios will wreck serious havoc with China's marriage markets in the not-too-distant future. The ratios start looking very skewed around 1985, which means that the impact will not really begin to be felt until after 2005. Note that the increasing skewed ratios over time means that looking for younger women will *not* be an option. It will be fascinating to watch this play out. If forced to speculate, we could say that there will be some strong pressure for sex-specific pro-immigration policies around 2010 in China. (The rise of an active gay culture during this time is practically a "predetermined element.")

[3]Yi Z. et al., "Causes and Implications of the Recent Increase in the Reported Sex Ratio at Birth in China," *Population and Development Review*, June 1993: 283–303.

Exhibit 5. Pruning the Family Tree: The Exponential Importance of Siblings

△	Female
○	Male
—	Direct relationship

Three generations of one-child families
(1980 Rural Fertility Rate)

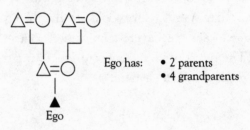

Ego has:
- 2 parents
- 4 grandparents

Three generations of three-child families
(1996 Urban Fertility Rate)

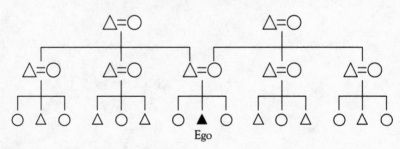

Ego

Ego has:
- 2 parents
- 2 siblings
- 4 grandparents
- 4 aunts
- 4 uncles
- 12 first cousins
- 24 first cousins, once removed
- 36 second cousins
- 4 grand aunts
- 4 grand uncles

Together, this chart tells a very stylized story about how different life is under a fertility regime of one-child versus three-children families over time. These pictures assume that everyone gets married and has exactly one child (or three children) for three generations, for simple purposes of illustration.

The result is striking: With one-child families (the prevailing fertility regime in China's urban areas today), an individual has a family network of just two parents and four grandparents to draw upon. By contrast, with three-child families (the prevailing rural fertility rate as recently as 1980), an individual has: two siblings; two parents; four grandparents; twelve first cousins; four grand-uncles; four grand-aunts; twenty-four first cousins, one generation removed (children of your great uncles and aunts, including their spouses); and thirty-six second cousins (children of your first cousins, once removed, *not* counting their spouses).

The "immediate" family network (tracing through grand-parents and their siblings) from the one-child families is six people; from the three-child families, it is eighty-eight persons (or twenty-eight, if you exclude the grandparents' siblings and their offspring).[4]

The implications of this shift are far-reaching. In his book on the economic implications of "the radius of trust" in different cultures, political philosopher Francis Fukuyama has documented the tremendous importance of family networks in Chinese economic development and job markets. A society of three-child families and a society of one-child families are entirely different worlds.[5]

One interesting, large-scale study of only children in China found that they had significantly better test scores on math and

---

[4]For instructions on how to draw kinship charts, go to: http://spirit.lib.uconn.edu/ArchNet/Topical/Educat/anth220/Kinkey.htm
For U.S. kinship term definitions (such as "first cousin, once removed"), go to: http://ic.net/~goroke/relation.htm
[5]Fukuyama, F., *Trust: The Social Virtues and the Creation of Prosperity*. New York: Free Press, 1995.

language skills but had no discernible negative emotional and psychological side effects (for example, there was no "little emperor," spoiled-brat syndrome).[6] To the extent that this is true, it may be an important source of competitive advantage for China in the future. Or, if you prefer the birth-order determinist view, one could use Frank Sulloway's recent book, *Born to Rebel* (Vintage Books, 1997), to speculate that a nation dominated by first-borns and only children will be a very conservative bunch (even if smarter).[7]

[6]Poston, Jr., D. and T. Falbo, "Scholastic and Personality Characteristics of Only Children and Children With Siblings in China," *International Family Planning Perspectives*, June 1990: 45–48.

[7]Sulloway, F. J. *Born to Rebel: Birth Order, Family Dynamics, and Creative Lives.* New York: Vintage Books, 1997.

Exhibit 6. Live Long and Prosper: Chinese Lifespan Adds Thirty Years in Less Than a Half-Century

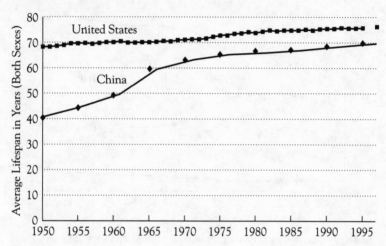

Source: United Nations, *World Population Prospects: The 1996 Revision;* World Bank, *World Development Indicators 1999.*

This really is an amazing transformation in lifespan improvement—much faster than was the case in historical United States or Europe. It is also important to note that China's lifespan today is almost identical to the United States, despite a much lower level of GDP per capita. Finally, China's average lifespan of forty years in 1950 does not mean that people were typically dying at age forty. Rather, most of the gains in life expectancy from ages forty to sixty can be traced to reductions in infant and child mortality (which skew the average severely downwards in high-mortality regimes).

Exhibit 7. China Comes of Age: Working-Age Adults Dominate Age Structure to 2020

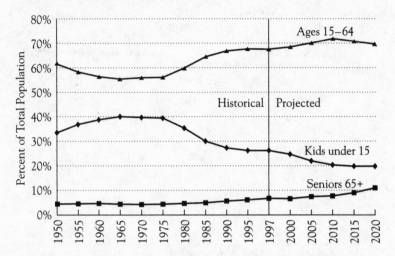

Source: United Nations, *World Population Prospects: The 1996 Revision;* World Bank, *World Development Indicators 1999.*

It is very important to keep in mind that in the early stages of fertility decline (for example, for the first generation, or thirty years or so), the term "population aging" really means that the nation's demographic profile shifts from children to adults. In China, as in other developing nations, the proportion of the population over age sixty-five is still very small (about 6 percent, compared to 15 percent in Japan) and will grow only slowly for many years to come. Rather, in the early decades of fertility decline, what occurs is that the overall dependency burden of children plus seniors falls sharply—creating a major advantage for the nation as a whole in terms of generation of savings available for investment.

Exhibit 8. The Competitive Advantage of Adults: Chinese Workers Supported Fewest Kids and Elderly Combined Among Ten Largest Developing Nations in 1996

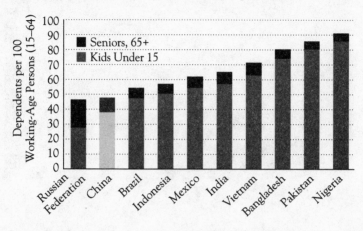

Source: Population Reference Bureau, 1996 World Population Data Sheet, World Bank, World Development Indicators 1999.

As this chart shows, China's unparalleled rapid fertility decline gives it a dependency ratio smaller than any other large developing nation (at 49.3 kids and seniors per 100 working-age persons). This will be an important competitive advantage for China for many years to come. Although Russia is "tied" with China in this graph, note that much more of Russia's dependents are elders (who are far more expensive than kids). Moreover, this advantage should persist over time for reasons that should be clear from Exhibit 7, on the previous page.

Both the United Nations and World Bank use ages fifteen to sixty-four as the "working age" population, since labor force participation rates (including informal work for family establishments, and so on) are typically quite high as early as age fifteen in developing countries such as China.

**Exhibit 9. A Nation of Savers:
China's Savings Rate Highest Among
Ten Largest Developing Nations in 1995**

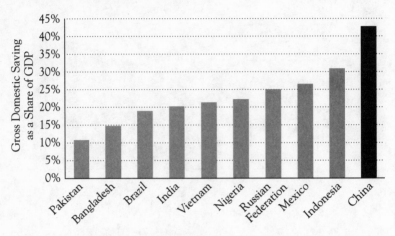

Source: World Bank, 1999 *World Development Indicators.*

Here is what you get with a nation dominated by working-age adults: the highest savings rates in the developing world. Of course, values come into play here, too. But thrift alone cannot account for a Chinese saving rate of over 42 percent of GDP—this just would not be possible with huge numbers of kids or seniors to support.

Exhibit 10. The Bright City Lights:
Slowly but Steadily Attract China's Rural Population

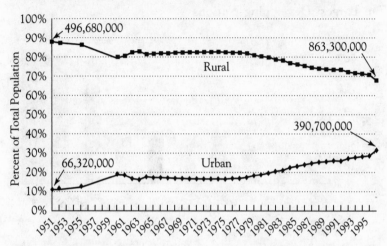

Source: *China Population Statistics Yearbook 1996*, World Bank, *World Development Indicators, 1999*.

The most striking fact in this graph is just how slowly China is urbanizing—to less than 30 percent urban by 1995 (far less than many developing countries, as the following exhibit shows).

**Exhibit 11. Still Among the Most Rural Nations:
Level of Urbanization Varied Widely Among
Ten Largest Developing Nations**

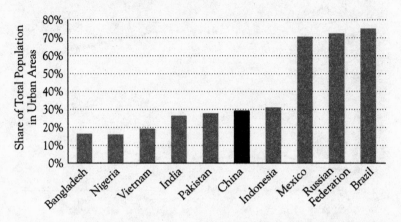

Source: Population Reference Bureau, 1996 World Population Data Sheet.

What is most striking about this exhibit is the wide variance of proportion of population that is urban in the ten largest developing nations. While China is about "average" among this group, the distribution is so skewed in a bimodal fashion that it makes little sense to speak in terms of averages. Rather, it is fair to say that the large developing nations fall into two broad groups: primarily rural and primarily urban. Clearly, China falls into the former category.

Exhibit 12. Of Showers and TVs:
The Personal Priorities of Development

	Color TVs per 100 households	Showers per 100 households
National	89.79	30.05
Beijing	113.60	45.40
Tianjin	101.80	30.20
Hebei	92.56	26.10
Shanxi	86.23	8.70
Inner Mongolia	84.22	7.33
Lianing	90.50	30.75
Jilin	85.49	21.87
Heilongjiang	82.90	13.57
Shanghai	108.60	36.60
Jiangsu	85.22	30.80
Zhejiang	95.76	47.28
Anhui	79.77	23.95
Fujian	90.36	43.24
Jiangxi	75.51	29.58
Shandong	90.55	23.93
Henan	84.01	17.98
Hubei	84.90	26.06
Hunan	86.80	35.90
Guangdong	104.97	74.60
Guangxi	78.17	45.76
Hainan	90.10	22.20
Sichuan	96.46	51.46
Guizhou	85.16	19.03
Yunnan	90.13	41.43
Tibet	n.a.	n.a.
Shaanxi	89.57	19.68
Gansu	90.48	15.55
Qinghai	94.00	6.89
Ningxia	99.10	25.23
Xinjiang	85.50	32.46

Source: China Statistical Yearbook, 1996 (Table 9–14).

This table serves two purposes: as a rough indicator of the uneven nature of development in China in general; and as a lesson in the personal priorities of development. It is very instructive to note just how much more common color television sets are than showers all throughout China.

Nancy Chen, a professor of anthropology at University of California-Santa Cruz who has done extensive fieldwork in rural China, comments:

> Most people don't have Western-style baths or showers, although this is changing for upper-middle-class homes. In urban areas the work units or municipality would have public baths where people had tickets to go once a week for free or more often for a fee. In rural areas a large aluminum bowl or sometimes tub would be used. In the urban apartments that I have seen, some families have small tubs about three feet oval shaped (like a horse trough) and they might have a shower tank with a hand-held shower head. The shower would heat up the water, which often posed electrocution problems with misuse or scalding problems if the water overheated. So all in all, most people still go to the public showers or if their work unit has a shower, they take showers there. I remember all the doctors and nurses at the hospital where I worked would take showers every Thursday when there was hot water for them.

Black Air, Gray Water

*The degree of environmental degradation in China is
serious. Rivers such as the Suzhou Creek are
anoxic—unable to sustain any form of life. Air
pollution, especially during the winter in cities such as
Lanzhou, can cause the sky to go black. The levels of
pollution particles were known to reach 1000 micrograms per cubic metre in some cities in the early
1980s, whereas London normally has forty-eight
and Tokyo twenty-two micrograms. There had
been cases when vegetables sold in the markets of
cities such as Shenyang had to be destroyed because
they were found to have contained heavy metals
beyond acceptable standards. Noise levels in cities
consistently exceed Chinese standards.*

from Patterns of China's Lost Harmony,
by Richard Louis Edmonds

Some Chinese cities are so swathed in smog that they become
virtually invisible on satellite photographs for long periods. One 1993
study estimated that air pollution causes some 915,000 premature
deaths each year in China—including the deaths of 300,000 children. The children born during the Cultural Revolution, when Mao
encouraged large families to build up China, are in the middle of their
reproductive years, so that even if China's one-child policy succeeds
in cutting the birth rate, conservative estimates put China's population at 1.4 billion by 2015. Of the 1,066 lakes in Hubei Province in
1949, only 326 still exist and their area has declined by 75 percent.
Forty percent of urban drinking water supplies are considered sub-
standard, 82 percent of surface waters are polluted, and Chinese
experts estimate that 450 of the 600 largest cities will be short of
water by 2000. Unfortunately, development is concentrated in the
Southeast, the region that holds 92 percent of China's arable land.

China faces an overwhelming environmental conundrum: The party heads in Beijing must maintain a great pace of economic growth in order to preserve domestic peace and their own hold on power—but fast-paced development and a burgeoning population throw off more pollution than the country (or the globe) can possibly sustain. In *China's Environmental Crisis* (M.E. Sharpe, Inc., 1993), Vaclav Smil argues that technological and institutional remedies cannot possibly accomplish enough, fast enough, to avoid a colossal environmental meltdown, with tragic results for China and the world.

If Belgium or Belize were to develop such horrible environmental problems, it would be a problem. When China does it, it becomes a global problem, a major sickness of the global environment. China has environmental laws—notably the Environmental Protection Law of 1989—just like it has laws that guarantee free speech and a free press and make it a crime to rape Tibetan nuns.

The worst sign is that, though some of the energy companies see the problems, many multinational corporations do not take them seriously yet. The most optimistic sign, on the other hand, is that many Chinese leaders are seeing the impact of environmental degradation on their children and grandchildren. For them, the problem is not about anything as abstract as sacred nature or Mother Earth, or about carrying capacity, or even about the environment as a bottleneck for the economy; it is about environmental diseases in their families.

The environment is a big uncertainty in the Chinese future: Will its rampant destruction throttle the economy? Will new technologies and a different attitude toward development solve the problem before then?

Chips and Fiber

China enters its industrial revolution in a post-industrial era. Today's leading-edge technologies not only offer many new opportunities to Chinese entrepreneurs, they offer new ways of organizing work that may fit the Chinese landscape and culture better than traditional industrial modes.

For instance, the largest-single foreign investor in China is Charoen Pokphand (CP), an agribusiness giant owned by a Thai Chinese family. Its biggest business is raising and processing chickens. Because of China's poor transport system, it has chosen to locate scores of small factories throughout the country—twenty-six of China's thirty provinces have at least one, and in the mid-1990s CP was averaging five new units a year. It would not be possible to manage such a widely distributed empire of relatively small business units without the efficiencies of modern telecommunications.

Similarly, the choke-point represented by China's growing hunger for energy could be loosened through a proliferation of new energy possibilities, distributed energy sources such as gas turbines, wind farms, fuel cells, and, in mountainous regions, small-scale hydroelectric.

Small, smart, local, networked uses of technology could make a great difference in solving the myriad problems that stand between China's present and its promising future.

Finally, today's communications technologies have a tendency to "tame" Beijing's urges toward rogue behavior by hooking all of China directly into the world communications net. In the 1990s, talk radio, fax machines, cell phones, the Internet, and cable and satellite TV have flowed around Beijing's attempts to control them. At one point, while Beijing had outlawed the sale of satellite dishes, another government agency continued to crank them out for sale—only now they were under the table, and they cost more. The coming satellite cell phones and modems will contribute to the porosity of China's information membrane.

With such a plethora of sources, it is unlikely that the Beijing government will ever again be able to so thoroughly control the minds of its people as it once did. During the Great Leap Forward, the Party propaganda machine wrote about such wonders of production as fields of wheat growing so densely that you could roll a baby atop the tassels of wheat, and still the stalks would not bend. And people believed what they heard. During the famine, the government said that rice steamed twice as long was twice as nutritious, and all over China, people steamed their rice twice as long and grew vats of "black tea fungus" that the government said was nutritious. In the 1990s (and increasingly in the new century), people can see what the rest of the world is like, they can experience realities not mediated by the government or the Party—and they can get their own messages out to the world.

The People's Liberation Army (PLA)

The largest single economic force in China, as well as one of the major political forces, is China's military, the People's Liberation Army (PLA). The PLA does not compare with, for example, the U.S. Army. For one thing, it includes the equivalent to the U.S. Air Force, Navy, Marines, and Coast Guard, plus the country's National Guards and Air National Guards, police forces and sheriff departments, and the Army Corps of Engineers, with NASA and the Border Patrol thrown in for good measure. The PLA also includes the Chinese arms industry, plus an array of businesses, from golf courses to flower shops, that have nothing to do with national defense.

According to David Shambaugh, a British military expert, the official budget of the PLA grew by 50 percent in real terms between 1988 and 1994, to an estimated $7 billion. But the "off-budget" profit generated by its many businesses—foreign arms sales, manufacturing, resort hotel complexes joint-ventured with foreign investors, and even special service deals with local governments— grew even faster, reaching $38 billion by 1993. The U.S. Arms Control and Disarmament Agency put the PLA's total 1996 budget at US$52 billion, behind only Russia and the United States, well ahead of Japan, and nearly five times that of Taiwan.

The PLA cuts a large silhouette on the world stage as the leading supplier of conventional, nuclear, and ballistic technology to

The Internet in China

China made its first network connection in 1993. By the following year all the universities were wired. By 1996, an Internet craze was sweeping China, with connection kits selling like crazy. Four hundred thousand legal copies and even more pirated copies of Bill Gates's *The Road Ahead* leapt off the shelves.

By early 1997, 86 percent of Chinese citizens had still never laid hands on a computer keyboard, but 1.6 percent of Chinese households owned one, and 4.1 percent planned to—small percentages by U.S. standards, but still up to 20 million potential sales. One hundred-fifty thousand people had personal connections to the Internet.

As is its style, the government has built a "Net Wall" (*wangguan*) that filters out unwanted information by searching for suspicious keywords. But given the vastness of the Internet, its goals are necessarily modest. As one public security functionary explained to *Wired* reporters Geremie R. Barmé and Sang Ye, "What we're particularly concerned about is material aimed at undermining the unity and sovereignty of China (that is, references to Tibetan independence and the Taiwan question), attempts to propagate new religions like the Children of God, and dissident publications. Commonplace ideological differences of opinion are now generally ignored" ("The Great Firewall of China," June 1997).

the developing world. The PLA's role in international arms deals, and the technology transfer associated with such deals, is a constant irritant to United States–China relations.

The PLA is a huge force, with the world's third-largest array of nuclear weapons and nearly 3 million men under arms. But some have called it the world's largest military museum. It has traditionally been undertrained and undergunned. But it is gaining rapidly in sophistication, and it is building a state-of-the-art, high-speed communications system. At the same time, it has acquired mid-air refueling capability (which allows bombers to strike at longer range) and a number of Sukhoi–27 Russian fighters (faster and stronger than anything Taiwan has), as well as the ability to manufacture an advanced version of the American F–16, based on the Israeli Lavi.

The PLA is building a blue-water navy capable of projecting force in the Pacific and Indian Oceans, and it has acquired two small "listening post" bases on Burmese territory on the Bay of Bengal and the Andaman Sea. Its planners speak of building "quick strike" air and naval ability and, indeed, have apparently put together a highly trained and heavily armed "rapid reaction force" of as many as 500,000 soldiers. Finally, and ominously, some authorities say that the Chinese appear to have built intercontinental ballistic missiles (named Dongfeng 5—"East Wind") capable of delivering nuclear weapons to any country in the world, including the United States.

At the same time, Chinese military planners recognize that the world is in the midst of a revolution in military affairs. In the future, one may not actually need to attack the U.S. Seventh Fleet or divisions of the Russian Far East Command. Instead, communications nodes, fiber-optic cables, and spy satellites would be destroyed. It may be possible in the future for some nation to be a major, yet unconventional, military power. But there is a problem with unconventional military means: They do not make a great parade. One cannot steam software hackers or satellite-killing lasers into the Formosa Straits or the Straits of Hormuz. One cannot array them impressively along the border to make a point. They have little symbolic power.

And symbolic power is of great importance to the Chinese. A military buildup does not necessarily mean that China has designs on anyone in particular. It does mean that they see military power as part of being a great power in the world. The ultimate persuader, when the United States is arguing its interests around the world, is its overwhelming military power and its willingness to use it—demonstrated just often enough to keep the threat credible.

Within China, the PLA's role as a counterforce to the Communist Party, as kingmaker or as spoiler, remains a major question in any future scenario. On the world stage, the emergence of China as a major military power of at least regional importance will shift and strain power relations all over East Asia.

Communist Party

Belief in Maoism, in Marxism, in struggle sessions and the "dictatorship of the proletariat," has evaporated from China like so much magician's smoke, leaving behind the Chinese Communist Party with its 58 million members (late 1997 figure). Deng is dead, Mao is long dead, the last of the nonagenarians who took the Long March with him are slipping into dusky death—and what is left?

The surprising fact is that the Chinese Communist Party, which was built around a fiery ideology and that fought for that ideology until it gained absolute power over the largest nation in the world, does not need that ideology to survive and maintain power. It needs results.

As long as average Chinese continue to feel better off than in recent memory, and feel reasonably safe in their homes, families, choices, and possessions, the Communist Party's hold on power is probably safe.

Besides an economic crisis, the greatest threat to Communist power is the succession problem. The Party has only the weakest constitutional means for handing down power, means that have been repeatedly shown to be impotent. In its seventy-five-year history, struggles for control of the party have repeatedly led to the purging and even murder of leaders, to factional warfare and chaos—the worst thing for a rapidly emerging China.

Even before Deng's death, intraparty struggles broke out over whether to expand his reforms or restrain them. One weapon of the struggle was classically Chinese: the essay. In 1996, hard-liner Deng Liquan circulated a "Ten Thousand Character Essay" calling for a return of the class struggle, this time against the *nouveau bourgeoisie* of China. At the same time, Cao Siyuan, a reformist purged in the aftermath of Tiananmen Square, argued that the Party could only hope to keep its grip on power if it continued the reforms, maintained economic growth, and kept its nose out of people's lives. But he could only get his essay published in a little-known provincial economics journal.

However, it is notable that China's leadership survived the death of Deng Xiaoping in February 1997 very well. There were no open and serious power struggles over the succession, such as many in the West had predicted; Jiang Zemin succeeded in consolidating his power as the General Secretary at the Fifteenth Party Congress in September 1997. The unpopular Premier Li Peng fulfilled the two terms the Chinese Constitution allowed him and, in March 1998, retired in favor of economic tsar Zhu Rongji. The Jiang-Zhu duumvirate appears quite suitable for leading China into the twenty-first century. As of mid-1999, China seems a model of political stability when compared with several of its neighboring countries.

In the meantime, being a Party member no longer means endless politicking over ideological purity, hounded by the possibility of humiliation and even death if you lose. Now it means being a member of the largest and most powerful web of *guanxi* in China. The Communist elite have not hung back from making money in any lingering fondness for Mao's principles, but instead have plunged right in, especially those whose public office gives them special power or insider information. The most vigorous New Capitalists have been the sons and daughters of the leadership, whom the Chinese call the *taizi*, or the "princes." *Taizi* such as Deng Pufang and Deng Zhifang, sons of Deng Xiaoping; and Larry Yung, son of former vice president Rong Yiren, have used their massive *guanxi* to accumulate fortunes as rapidly as possible. It is this class favoritism and crass greed that seem more than anything else to embitter Chinese about the Party.

But bitterness, even mockery, do not destroy power. The real questions are whether China's rulers can keep the economy growing, and whether the party can maintain a cohesive identity as other influences flood China and other organizations grow—or whether it will fall apart in a morass of ugliness and greed.

The "Class of '77"

When Deng died, global news media throbbed with speculation over one question: Who would be the new maximum leader, the next "Red Emperor"? But the truly important question might well be: What do we know about the new generation of Chinese poised to take leadership at all levels, in the government, the universities, the army, and in business? The answer to this question is good news for China and, ultimately, for the world.

Just when it looks like China will need a steady, enlightened, well-connected leadership, a new generation is reaching its prime. Nicknamed the "Class of '77," after the first class to graduate from the universities after Mao's death, this generation is far different from Deng's generation, or even Li Peng's. This generation has no memory of a China run by warlords and landlords, but it does have a deep, searing memory of China in a chaos caused by radical politicians. During the Cultural Revolution, many of this generation of educated, urban, young people were forced into the countryside as members of Red Guard units or to work with the peasants in rice paddies, in machine shops, or on construction crews. This generation has, like Mao's generation, an intimate acquaintance with the lives of the people of the countryside. But unlike their predecessors, this generation is highly educated, often with degrees from foreign universities. As a generation, it has a great deal of experience with the world beyond China.

The Flea and the Elephant

When Margaret Thatcher signed an accord that agreed to return Hong Kong to China at the end of its lease on July 1, 1997, the

leaders of the island colony placed what seemed at the time an
extraordinary bet—that they could transform China before China
could transform Hong Kong, that they could help shift China a
huge distance toward being an open, capitalistic powerhouse.

By the time of the turnover, the Hong Kong elite had wrought
remarkable changes on China, particularly on Guangdong
Province, just beyond its borders. Hong Kong had poured over
US$100 billion in investments and another US$42 billion in loans
into the Chinese economy—nearly 60 percent of all foreign investment. Guangdong, which had been a verdant countryside of rice
paddies, dirt paths, and mud-brick villages, had sprouted instant
cities such as Daliang and Shenzen, freeways, and curtain walls of
gleaming office buildings, apartments, and warehouses. It had
flooded Guangdong, and China beyond it, with videos, neon, rock
music, kung fu flicks, and Mercedes. It had drawn millions of poor
rural Chinese out of the deep interior to work in the factories, warehouses, and shops of the south coast.

Beijing clearly wanted to learn something from a city-state
with a GDP per capita ten times the size of its own, and it had
promised to let Hong Kong keep its own system after the handover. But the system that Hong Kong had at the time that Beijing made the promise was in many respects much like its
own—an authoritarian, appointed government that allowed for
little dissent and a muzzled if nominally free press. It had never
promised to let Hong Kong keep the democratic elections and
party politics that the colony suddenly sprouted in the 1990s. In
the years running up to the handover, Hong Kong Chinese split
into two camps—roughly, those who thought they could work
with Beijing and those who thought the situation called for firm
resistance. Beijing, of course, appointed a government made completely of the first group.

Even the pro-Beijing party, though, professed a strong attachment to free speech and an open political process. Some projected
a vision of a future Hong Kong as the safety valve of China, the

vent city, the place where dissidents were shipped to when Beijing had had enough of them.

Although Hong Kong suffered economic crisis in the first years of Chinese rule, this was not because of, but despite the fact that it had become a part of China. It was caught up in the financial and economic crisis that affected the region. Contrary to the expectations of many in the West, the Chinese leaders continued to allow demonstrations of protest against the Tiananmen Square Massacre. When the strongest of anti-Beijing politicians won elections in mid-1998 for the Hong Kong legislature, the new leaders applauded the fact that so many people had shown up to vote and made no attempt to prevent them from taking their seats. Despite a good beginning in the first year and more of Beijing's rule, it will take much longer to know just who won what prize in this face-off. The flea will have a disproportionate effect on the elephant. Beijing may, in fact, learn what it hoped and feared it would learn: that democracy is the necessary hand-maiden of free market capitalism, and that the free flow of ideas, opinions, and votes enhances the free flow of commerce.

Who's the Bully?

As China bulks up, its economy growing, its armed forces modernizing and expanding, other world players get nervous. As China scholar Kenneth Lieberthal put it in 1996:

> The People's Republic of China has been in the news this year for a number of disturbing reasons. It has mounted muscular military actions to back its diplomacy regarding Taiwan and the South China Sea, allegedly transferred M–11 missile technology to Pakistan, sold nuclear technology to Iran, conducted nuclear weapons tests, and augmented its military budget when most countries have been cutting back in the wake of the Cold War.

Taiping Rebellion

If the extraordinary excesses of China's history in the twentieth century—revolutions, famines, massacres, invasion, explosive economic growth—do not quite convince you of China's capacity to surprise, consider a piece of its nineteenth-century history.

China had been ruled by foreigners, Manchus, since 1644. In 1850, the Manchu Qing Dynasty was already reeling under the incursions of foreign powers and the British victory in the Opium War. In Fuyuan-shui, a small village in Guangdong, the local schoolteacher, Hong Xiuquan, was trying to better himself by passing the Imperial examinations, the time-honored route to a good job in the government bureaucracy. He failed and returned home in humiliation. He took to his bed in a fever. After three days of delirium he woke to reveal that he had been given a vision: He was the second Son of God, Jesus's younger brother, and he had been sent to save China.

Surprisingly, his family and friends mostly believed him. One friend organized a God Worshippers Society in his honor. When the local police units came after them, Hong and his followers fled and joined bands of robbers in the mountains of Guangxi. The robbers, too, were converted.

Still, China's military is far smaller, compared to the size of its population, the length of its borders (with fourteen neighbors), and the size of its land mass, than that of most other major countries. And we can build an equally long list of recent peace-making actions— settling its border problems with India, and establishing full relations with Indonesia, South Korea, and Singapore.

If China's military seems more restive than we are used to, it is in contrast to centuries in which China was turned inward—first by the decay of the Qing, then by nearly forty years of continual civil war and invasion, then by a Communist military and political stance.

If China were to exercise all the territorial claims that have as much merit as its claim to Tibet (claims, for example, backed by

In 1851, Hong adopted the title of *Tian-wang* (Heavenly King) and declared a new dynasty named *Taiping Tianguo* (Heavenly Kingdom of Great Peace). He came down from the mountains and swiftly gained adherents as he swept north through the verdant valley of the Yangtze. Soldiers, farmers weakened by famine, poor workers, and miners flocked to his banner. He preached a primitive communism, land reform, prayer, and an abstemious lifestyle that included strict separation of the sexes, though he himself kept a harem. By the time he got to Nanking, the Heavenly King had a million followers.

He took Nanking, tried and failed to take Beijing, and was turned back at Shanghai by a private army with Western officers. Squabbling in the top ranks led to executions and schism, but with his hard core of believers, he held Nanking and much of southern China for thirteen years. He was only defeated finally when the Manchu turned the leadership of the army over to Chinese officers. Over 100,000 followers of the Heavenly King chose death rather than surrender. The Way of Heavenly Peace had cost more than 20 million lives.

Though the Qing tottered on for nearly another half-century, the Taiping rebellion was the beginning of the end. The Qing had shown that they had lost the mandate of heaven, and they were doomed.

several centuries of occupation), it would reconquer not only Taiwan, but Mongolia, almost half of Kirgizstan, a substantial bite out of Kazakhstan, a piece of Siberia southwest of Lake Balkash, and the most populous part of the Russian Far East, including Vladivostok.

But China has not recently been a militarily expansive culture. As opposed to, for example, Japan, the United States, or the major European countries, China essentially reached its present borders in the Tang dynasty (618–907) nearly fourteen centuries ago, and has not engaged in any real military expansion for over two centuries. Since 1949, China has shown itself willing to use military force to back its opinions about border questions, to defend itself, to put down rebellions, and in one case to punish a neighbor—but never to invade or subjugate another country. In Korea, Chinese military planners felt they were reacting to a direct and credible military threat to their industrial heartland in Manchuria and to Beijing itself. The Vietnam incursion of 1979 was a "punishment" rather than a conquest.

Traditionally, whether under emperors, Nationalists, or Communists, the main task of the military has been to control the population and put down rebellions, and the second task has been to protect against invasion. Unlike most modern nations (the United States in its drive for Manifest Destiny, Moscow in its drive for a warm-water port and buffer space against Europe, London in its drive for the Empire), China has had few national interests beyond its borders—though that could change if it becomes energy-starved and feels cut off from the sources that it needs.

To stay at peace with a defensive country, do not do things that cause it to feel driven into a corner, surrounded, trapped. From Beijing's point of view, it is the West, especially the United States, that is the bully, picking on China, interfering with its internal affairs in Tibet and Taiwan and in arguments over human rights. Already nationalistic sentiments are building in China. To many in the West, this point of view may seem insupportable, but the West's opinion does not count. If China feels bullied and trapped, it will react with ferocity. It will become the pit bull that we have made it in our nightmares.

The United States

The United States is the world's largest economic and military force. It has long thought of itself as having a special relationship to China, a strange mix of missionary spiritual aspirations, economic ties, and political opinions.

Perhaps even more important to the future of both China and the world, the United States is the guarantor, either by treaty or practice, of peace in the region and the fragile balance of power on which that peace is built. Of China's immediate neighbors on the

Pacific, the United States has direct military alliances with Japan and South Korea, a half-century-old, god-fatherly relationship with Taiwan, and a ticklish but still close relationship with the Philippines. China has disputes or potential disputes with three of these neighbors and a claim of total sovereignty over the fourth.

As long as China was neutered by self-absorption and poverty, these were not great concerns. As China rapidly gains in power and wealth, the situation rapidly grows more unstable.

The United States has waded hip-deep into Chinese politics for over a century, sending troops in to help quell the Boxer Rebellion in 1900, demanding that Chiang Kai-shek turn over command to "Vinegar Joe" Stilwell in 1943, using American troops to help Chiang against Mao in 1945, trading away bits of Chinese sovereignty over Manchuria at Yalta, and preventing Mao from pursuing Chiang across the Formosa Straits. We have consistently held the rather arrogant view that if we could just impose our way on these people, everything would be fine.

The United States has consistently misunderstood China, through both Chinese manipulation and American ignorance. For decades, Americans generally pictured Chiang as a Jeffersonian democrat. Throughout the 1940s, American diplomats in their private dispatches consistently pictured Mao and his followers as "agrarian reformers," and democrats as well. During the Great Leap Forward, Western reporters and diplomats reporting from inside China consistently and explicitly denied that there was any famine to be found in China.

The United States has consistently exaggerated its impact on China. The McCarthyism of the early 1950s was fueled in part by vicious polemics over "Who lost China?"—as if China was ours to lose. The same exaggeration of our own powers fuels today's debate over human rights. When President Bill Clinton visited China in June and July 1998, the Western press exaggerated his impact on Chinese society enormously. Many suggested, for instance, that his visit had forced the Chinese leaders to take democratic ideas seri-

Would the U.S. Go to War for Taiwan?

The United States has no predatory designs on For-mosa [Taiwan]. . . . Nor does it have any intention of utilizing its armed forces to interfere in the present situa-tion. The United States Government will not pursue a course that will lead to involvement in the civil conflict in China.

—Harry Truman, January 5, 1950

In these circumstances, the occupation of Formosa by Communist forces would be a direct threat to the security of the Pacific area and to the United States forces . . . in that area.
—Harry Truman, June 27, 1950, in ordering the Seventh Fleet to defend Taiwan from the Communists, two days after North Korea invaded South Korea.

Ever since Harry Truman, American presidents have been sending the Seventh Fleet to steam the Formosa Straits, rattling sabres over the defence of Taiwan. Ever since Douglas MacArthur, American politicians and generals have been pounding the lectern and jabbing the air in their determination to make it clear that the United States would defend Taiwan from invasion by the People's Republic of China. For decades, Beijing has been stating categorically that if Taiwan declared independence, the People's Liberation Army would invade. Clearly this has long been a flash point at the ready, capable of igniting a truly ugly and major war. And now that Hong Kong has been returned to Beijing's rule, the heat on the Taiwan question has turned up. As recently as Spring 1997, Speaker of the House Newt Gingrich stated categorically that the United States would go to war to defend Taiwan against Beijing.

Would we? The conventional wisdom says that we would. There are several reasons why we may not.

- Beijing is not Baghdad. Taiwan is now wildly democratic, and Beijing remains repressive, but there is no clear "Hitler" type running the government.

- Taiwan is not Kuwait, a tiny, helpless, nearly undefended country. Taiwan has 21 million citizens, with 365,000 of them under arms in one of the world's best-trained and best-equipped armed forces.

- China has nuclear weapons, with rockets that can deliver them to Taiwan as well as (according to some analysts) to the United States.

- There is no clear way to win, to stop Beijing from bombarding and attempting to invade Taiwan. Since Vietnam, the U.S. military has acquired a quite sensible allergy to wars that have no clear, achievable goal.

Altogether, it is not all that easy to argue to U.S. mothers that they should willingly send their children off to defend Taiwan. And yet, President Clinton, or his successor, or the president after that, may attempt to make just that argument.

Despite its large and well-trained military, Taiwan's greatest defense is the sheer difficulty of mounting an invasion across straits that are three times as wide as the English Channel. According to *San Francisco Chronicle* reporter Frank Viviano in a 1997 article called "Mainland Improves Its Military," one Chinese naval officer admitted to an American defense attaché that the only way Beijing could successfully invade Taiwan "would be with the help of the U.S. Navy."

Of course, the ultimate defense is not to need one. Taiwan's greatest safety lies in the hope that both sides know that the massive destruction of a modern war would not only cause great harm, but would set back China's own development by a generation or more.

Japan and China

Why do so many Chinese hate and fear the Japanese? They shake their heads in wonder at the close relationship between Washington and Tokyo. The Americans, they say, just don't understand.

What don't we understand? History. Americans fought the Japanese a half-century ago. The Chinese were invaded, most of them lived under Japanese occupation, and millions of Chinese remember it vividly.

The invasion and occupation started in 1931, when Japanese forces took Manchuria. The invasion spread to the rest of China in 1937, and only ended with Japanese surrender in 1945. At the height of this invasion, Japan had well over a million men in China, controlling virtually all of the eastern third of the country—which holds most of the population, all the ports, and most of the transportation and industry. And it was not gentle. In the notorious "Rape of Nanking," Japanese soldiers tied civilians up in large groups and used them for bayonet practice, or simply doused them with kerosene and set them on fire. They burned, raped, looted, terrorized, and molested at will. An International Relief Committee later documented more than 42,000 civilians killed by hand after the taking of Nanking, in addition to the tens of thousands killed by bombardment and other war actions. During the International War Crimes Tribunal held in Tokyo

ously for the first time. But processes leading in this direction had been going on for years. Clinton helped them, but he did not initiate them; the overall difference he made was no more than marginal.

What the United States thinks about China is important. What the United States does about China is deeply problematic. There are things that we can do that will make the situation a lot worse, but not a lot of things we can do to make it better. For instance, Japan has asked for a theater missile defense (TMD) system. If the after the war, the tales of Nanking—supported in part by snapshots taken by Japanese troops and turned in to Shanghai photo shops for processing—shocked even the war-jaded Japanese public. Nor was Nanking an isolated incident. At Baoding, for instance, the Japanese killed nearly 30,000 (and admitted it to American General Joseph Stilwell), then burned all the schoolbooks and library books and destroyed all the medical equipment.

Throughout Yangtze plain, and all across occupied China, Japanese soldiers torpedoed fishing junks, bombed and strafed civilians, mowed them down with machine guns, rained incendiary bombs on universities, burned towns, pillaged cities, and raped women. Counting civilian and military casualties, China lost an estimated 10 million people to the Japanese invasion.

In the decades since, China (along with other East Asian nations) has suggested repeatedly that Japan should apologize for its wartime depredations, or at least admit to them. China has stressed that Japan should change what it teaches its school children about the war. Until recently, Tokyo spurned all such suggestions—and recently has accepted them only grudgingly and partially.

Chinese business and political leaders recognize the need to get along with the Japanese, but they do not love them—and they do not understand why Americans seem to.

United States were to install TMDs in Japan, Beijing would likely regard the action as proof that the United States and Japan were carrying out a "containment" policy against China, as we did for decades against the Soviet Union. Beijing would likely respond by accelerating its own military buildup. And the cycle would have no clear offramp: We could help the Japanese rearm further (because the Chinese are building up), thus increasing Chinese paranoia, further stoking a general regional arms race, and possibly leading to the very war we hoped to forestall.

So far, modern China has never had a Hitler, a Napoleon, or a similar charismatic, nationalistic military leader bent on expunging China's fears and securing China's place in history through wars of domination. We could, if we are not careful, help create the conditions for such a leader to emerge.

The United States has not had a clear and consistent China policy for decades. In public at least, the center of our policy debates has been human rights, to the exclusion of almost every other consideration. More recently, "constructive engagement" has been the watchword. But incidents like the bombing of the Chinese embassy in Belgrade and the uncovering of Chinese spying on U.S. nuclear technology have undermined the "constructive" part of the "engagement." The situation calls for care, subtlety, and something approaching wisdom—and so far our cupboard is bare.

3

The Worms in the Core

Five big, hidden negatives have the power to keep China from becoming the powerhouse of the coming century.

The Massive Financial and Social Debt of the State-owned Enterprises

"The worm at the core" of China's economy (as author and economic analyst Jim Rohwer termed it) consists of an estimated 100,000 "state-owned firms." As late as the mid-1990s, they still employed 115 million workers (70 percent of the industrial workforce) and used some 75 percent of all assets, yet they generated only one-third of the country's industrial production, and a mere 1 percent of its profit. While steps have been taken to privatize many of the SOEs, solving the SOE problem just contributes to a further problem of unemployment.

The Deep-rooted Poverty of 350 Million Rural Citizens

Despite expenditures of around one billion dollars per year by the Chinese government, as of 1994 approximately 25 percent of China's population—350 million people—were still living in poverty, including 60 million still living at the near-starvation level of 60 cents per day or less. Particularly as the rich get gloriously richer, this lumpen proletariat has the makings of the next long march.

The Destruction of the Environment

The quality of China's land is declining rapidly because of soil erosion, overpopulation, overfarming, pollution, overdevelopment, and the growing salinity of delta farm lands. By some estimates, China has consumed 25 percent of her total forest just in the last thirty years, and one-seventh of the country is now desert. The Gobi, the great desert on China's north flank, is spreading at the rate of 950 square miles a year.

Lack of Adequate Infrastructure

China has coal for heat and electricity, but inadequate rail lines to transport the coal. Nor are there enough roads to transport products from inland manufacturing facilities. Phone lines are infamously in short supply, leading to the strong market for wireless phone and pager systems.

The "Level Playing Field" Problem

Corruption and the lack of an adequate legal system to enforce the rule of law

How do you put numbers on a lack? There is too little to count, too few printed laws, and, hard as it may be for Americans to contemplate, too few lawyers. The lack of a working legal system makes it hard for Westerners to do business. What we call corruption, they consider family values: Of course Mr. Li will favor his brother over a trader from Seattle. Nepotism is not a negative in Nanking; it is the way things work.

We will see these several worms working their way through the following scenarios. Whether or not China manages to join the world economy as an honored member and an equal among equals will depend in large part on how these worms wiggle their way into future history.

Part Two

Scenarios of the Future of China

Scenarios are alternative environments in which today's decisions may be played out. They are not predictions. Nor are they strategies. Instead they are descriptions of different futures specifically designed to highlight the risks and opportunities involved in specific strategic issues.

Scenarios can help overcome anxiety about the lack of hard evidence regarding the future because scenarios do not claim to be predictions. The point is not to gather evidence for some induction about a most probable future. The point is rather to entertain a number of different possibilities to better make reasoned choices among them.

We cannot know beforehand what the future will hold. So-called futurists cannot be seers. But we can see in the present several trends that, moving on their current course, will change the shape of China over the next decade. In order to think about the possible consequences of current trends, it is useful to create scenarios with specificity and detail. The danger of detail consists in allowing the plausibility of any one scenario to hinge on whether a given event happens or does not happen. The scenario genre therefore strikes a balance between offering enough detail to make a given future imaginatively compelling, but not so much that a scenario would be dismissed because a single event failed to occur.

In each of the following scenarios, different assumptions drive different logics. These scenarios are not based on a single model pushed faster or slower, higher or lower, optimistic or pessimistic, best case or worst case. Instead, we have explored different models of development, and we have invented characters and specific events to breathe dramatic life into those abstract models.

4

An Introduction to Scenarios and Development Models

China's changes and mushrooming economic growth in the 1990s have pumped new life into the venerable industry of writing about China, especially about its future. The flurry of books by fellow future-gazers has buried us in images of China's future. Yet for all their variety, these images settle out as variations on three basic "conventional wisdom" scenarios:

"Conventional Wisdom" Scenario 1: Singapore × 70

China succeeds in fashioning itself after Lee Kuan Yew's amazing Swiss-watch city-state. It becomes a disciplined, benign, tightly integrated economic powerhouse just like Singapore, only scores of times bigger.

"Conventional Wisdom" Scenario 2: Soviet Devolution

Like the Soviet Union, the People's Republic of China breaks up, either peacefully or violently, into four, six, or more pieces, some rich and some poor, but all impotent militarily and politically, consumed by rivalry and struggling with their interdependence.

"Conventional Wisdom" Scenario 3: The Big Bully

China reconstitutes itself not as a giant Singapore, but as a giant North Korea: belligerent, brutal, harshly centralized, and absolutist, sapping the life from Hong Kong, cracking down on the million capitalist experiments of Deng's legacy, bullying Taiwan, picking fights with its neighbors, exporting weaponry and discontent to the other rogue regimes of the world.

Surprising China

We think China will be more surprising than these conventional scenarios.

History in general is rarely neat. It follows underlying trends, but rarely in simple, straight lines. As GBN partner Stewart Brand once remarked to the authors, "Scenarios struggle under the constraint of plausibility. Unfortunately, reality doesn't."

Chinese history, in particular, shows a continuing ability to surprise. What astute observer of China in 1850 would have predicted the Taiping Rebellion that cracked the Qing Dynasty? In 1934, with Mao in seeming ignominious retreat in his "Long March," who would have predicted his unalloyed victory a mere fifteen years later? Or the twenty to thirty million who died in the "Great Leap Forward" of the late 1950s, or the several million more who died in the Cultural Revolution of the 1960s and 1970s? In 1976, watching the thousands file past Mao's bier, who would have predicted Deng Xiaoping's return to power in 1978, his extraordinary loosening of the rules under the startling slogan, "To get rich is glorious!" or the bumptious, brawling way the Chinese economy responded, becoming one of the world's fastest growing economies for the two decades since?

We have gone into the smoke and thunder of the great forces driving China into the future and come up with other scenarios, equally plausible, firmly grounded in the realities of the present, but outside of conventional thinking.

Developmental Models

Anyone who paints a vision of a future is using a model, a set of assumptions about how things work, especially about what makes a country cohere, and what makes an economy grow.

These are some of the common models:

- *Free markets, open societies, and an orientation toward exports lead to growth.* We can call this the "Washington consensus." It is the closest thing we have to a grand, unified consensus theory of economics. Beyond the core, it gets a lot fuzzier. There is no consensus, for instance, about whether you need technology, or democracy and a bill of rights, or good contract law and plenty of lawyers, or even whether interest rates should be high or low. Its major examples are Japan and the Asian "Tigers," such as Singapore, Taiwan, South Korea, and Hong Kong. It is behind the worldwide move toward free trade and the privatization of state-run economies.

- *Protecting domestic industry through trade barriers, supporting it with subsidies, and directing investment in it through government intervention, leads to growth.* This "London School of Economics model" was the previous heavyweight champion. The key phrase here is "import substitution," which means trying to make things in your own country instead of importing them from more developed ones—whether or not they are things you are particularly good at making, or have the resources for. This model drove the economic policies of much of the post-colonial developing world and almost all state-controlled communist and socialist economies over the last half-century—but cannot boast a single shining example of success.

- *Investment in infrastructure—dams, power plants, ports—leads to growth.* Call this the "World Bank model," as much of the World Bank's lending has traditionally made this assumption.

- *Keeping the "Mandate of Heaven" through wise government and proper attention to ritual leads to growth.* This "Confucian model" underlies the most common traditional Chinese view of the history of development in China. A number of other societies around the world consider themselves the "chosen people of God" and feel that they succeed only when they give proper attention to that relationship.

- *Having the right man in charge leads to growth.* Call this the "Great Man model." If you are led by Alexander, or Peter the Great, or Napoleon, you will do fine. If you are led by Ethelred the Unready, heaven help you. History supports this theory, but only in short bursts, and even then only by careful selection of data.

In each of our scenarios, a model underlies our assumptions. In our first scenario, for example, the underlying logic, the model, is that of a network.

The only organization capable of unprejudiced growth, or unguided learning, is a network.
— *Kevin Kelly,* Out of Control

Network-like organizational models share certain characteristics that allow for unmanaged hypergrowth. In this model, each node is responsible for itself, but all are allowed equal access to whatever they need to survive. In an economic model, that means markets, technology, capital, and labor. Our assumption is this: Maximize that access, take down the barriers, increase the communications, and you will get growth.

Kelly identifies a number of prescriptions derived from the behavior of networked organizations:

- Distribute decision-making: As far as possible, let control come from the bottom.

- Grow by chunking: Make a complex thing out of simple things that work.

- Have multiple goals: Setting a grand goal from above leads to distortions. The Great Leap Forward is a prime example.

- Let the rules change as they need to.

- Rely on local knowledge.

- Expect turbulence. "In turbulence is the preservation of the world."

The network model guides our first scenario. It will play an important role in our second scenario as well. However, there, in "The New Mandarins" scenario, Confucian hierarchy elevates the nodes of the network to a height from which different "great men" claim to implement "the mandate from heaven." In the third scenario, no model works. Aspirants to the Great Man model turn out to be villains, and darkness rules.

Our first two scenarios conclude with lists of scenario spoilers, and darker versions of what China might look like if the model driving the dominant scenario does not work. We look at the brighter and darker sides of uncertainty, but we explore more than one model of development. The third scenario does not conclude with scenario spoilers or a dark side because the entire scenario is spoiled and dark.

Like the rest of the world, China has its light and dark sides, its sources of strength and signs of weakness. Our portrait of China's possibilities explores several versions of success and failure, several models of growth and development or decay, several scenarios for China's futures.

5

Scenario One:
China Web

In this scenario, China builds a massively decentralized village-based economy linked by wireless telecommunication and efficient transport. The world's most massive agricultural nation finds a way to leapfrog the industrial revolution straight to the information age. To the surprise of the world's environmentalists, it builds a relatively clean economy, with just enough steel, coal, oil, and railroads to undergird the vast ramifying web linking Township and Village Enterprises (*xiangzhen qiye*) all over the country. These TVEs harness China's greatest resource, the energy of its billion peasants, to serve the economy of the new century.

China finds that it can modernize without industrializing or Westernizing. Rather than massive enterprises relying on economies of scale, China builds a massive, self-ramifying web of tiny enterprises at work.

Gujiang, Jiangxi Province, April 17, 2022

Gujiang is not what it was a quarter-century ago. The three old men in their neat silk suits in the teahouse on the square shake their heads and laugh at how strange it all is. One difference, of course, is that they can talk like this to a foreign researcher, with no one else around but the local interpreter, with no worries about what the officials will think. It has been slow to come, but finally, within reason, as long as they do not come right out and criticize the government, people can talk freely in China. Really, people would say with a shrug, what was to criticize?

But the biggest change is the simple fact that they are sitting in the teahouse in the middle of the day. They are retired. Gujiang has become so prosperous that the old people can sit and gossip, or play checkers, or plan their bus trip to Nanchang, the provincial capital. Beyond the square, the streets are lined with red-brick houses, none more than twenty years old, many of them two stories high. Cars and motorbikes clog the streets. The stores around the square are filled with goods from China and around the world. On one side of the square, the jade-green tiles and gold-leafed beam ends of the Wong Kwok Nai Temple, home to the town's fortune tellers, still sparkle from its lavish refurbishment a few years back. Young women in designer silk suits pass by, talking on tiny global cell phones.

"We used to hear about these things happening in Guangdong and Fujian," says one of the old men, in a jaunty checkered cap. "When we got television here, in 1995, we could see them. It started to happen here, a few people got rich. But now, it's everybody. The whole place is wonderful."

The elder on the other side of the table was a professorial sort, carrying a pipe. "The young people," he said, flinging an arm contemptuously at the twentyish waitress behind the counter, "they have no idea. They take it all for granted—the clothes, the good houses, even having enough to eat."

What has made the difference? All three of them turn, all talking at once, and gesture emphatically toward a three-story brick building just beyond the square. The characters on the building read "Gujiang #1 Town Enterprise Factory." Under the sign is a portrait of Deng, and a smaller sign reading, "All Praise To Paramount Leader Deng Xiaoping!"

"Of course, now there are six different buildings scattered around town," says the tiny, wizened elder in the middle.

"Of course," adds the man in the cap, "it's not really just the one enterprise. There are 200 businesses in those buildings and scattered all over town. A lot of people just work at home."

The third gestures, both hands up and palms out, then placed solidly down, as if on a lectern, and launches into a history of the place. "Around here, it really started in 1995. We started making shoes. Nikes. But everybody was doing that, so people started branching out. The town used some profits to buy new equipment, and we started stamping out CDs. They contracted out the labeling, printing, boxing, shipping, the whole thing, to different groups around town. Then a group of young men in town started learning to write software, so we gave them some space and bought some equipment, and kept buying more. They always had to have the latest, but it was worth it. By 1999, the biggest town enterprise was turning out network computers, remember those? That lasted about two years, then they got into Windows pads, those roll-up computers, and then the disposable computers, where you just keep the chip. Whatever the new thing was, we'd build it. Some towns got into dolls, or pens, or electric guitars, or hats. We did electronics, mostly."

"We had a committee to decide," the tiny man cut in.

"Not a committee, a team," the professor corrected him with a withering look. "The team would pick the next product and make the plans."

"But that was just for the biggest enterprises, the ones the town itself owned. Everybody does stuff themselves, or with a few friends or cousins. They can do whatever they want. The town will give them a small loan to start up."

What's the interest rate? "Not cheap," said the professor.

"Shouldn't be cheap," said the man in the cap. "People waste cheap money."

"Anyway, you lose face if you don't pay it back," said the tiny man. "Nobody goes bankrupt."

How do people get paid? "Several ways," said the professor. "Everyone in the village has a share in the factories the town owns, and their profits. And many people here have jobs with the factory, or working for a cousin or friend. And of course people get the profits from their own businesses. A lot of people do both. They work in the town factory or out in the fields, then they come home and work on their own business. It's not like in the old days, where you got paid no matter what you did. This is all piece work. The more you do, the more money you make. You make enough, you can take a vacation. Or retire. Like we did."

"All the ordering and the marketing and everything, it's all on the Net," said the second man, eager to recoup his place in the conversation. "And we don't design anything. We're just a little town. And we don't do the raw materials. We fabricate. We bring in the raw materials by truck from the airport in Ji'an, turn them into products, and send them back out."

Looking back to the turn of the century, we have to say that the Chinese got it right—here in Gujiang, and all across the country—in ways that no one at the time expected. A quarter-century ago, Western pundits had lists of what we thought of as problems for China, stumbling blocks in the way of its growth, including:

- Its million villages and massively rural population

- Income inequities between rural and urban areas, the coast and the interior

- The fear of chaos that drove it to authoritarian government

- The lack of a single strong leader after Deng Xiaoping

- The weakness of its physical infrastructure and heavy manufacturing

- The weakness or near-absence of any clear legal system or civil society to parallel and temporize government and business

- Its predilection for family- and village-sized enterprises,
  for familial over formal management, sacrificing
  economy of scale for control.

China did not merely solve those problems. It proved that they were strengths.

The idea of local enterprise itself was not new. Already in 1978, when Deng first trumpeted the glory of profit, China boasted 1.5 million *xiangzhen qiye*. By 1995, there were more than 22 million of them, employing about 130 million people and producing over three-quarters of China's total rural output value and nearly 20 percent of its total GDP. But once the Chinese leadership took the decision, in 1998, to grow a "distributed light industrial economy" on the roots of the *xiangzhen qiye*, things moved rapidly. In the late 1990s and early 2000s, TVEs sprang up across China "like bamboo after a spring rain," making everything from Barbie dolls to glass communication fibers. By 2010, there were nearly 40 million of these tiny enterprises, and their production had grown to 54 percent of the GDP. Today, further increases in productivity have pushed that to 78 percent and made China's web of TVEs the wonder economic story of the new century.

For the most part, Beijing had to do two things for this to take off: It had to provide the infrastructure, and it had to get out of the way.

China's state-owned enterprises were a special problem. In the late 1990s Beijing began breaking the grip of the state enterprises. Over a period of ten years, the central government slowly reduced their subsidies to zero, and demanded that they live off their profits. The government diverted the saved resources—and every resource it could harness from business through incentives and grants—into infrastructure: highways, railroads, ports, airports, power plants, telecommunications, as well as such "people investments" as healthcare and primary and secondary education. It cleared away the mass of party and government red tape and taxes that hobbled local enterprise and gave out small starter loans to buy equipment.

Despite the lack of strong leadership from a single figure, or guiding ideology—other than Deng Xiaoping's famous dictum "To get rich is glorious"—the Chinese have built the world's most successful economy on three supports:

• Decentralization

• The overriding pragmatism and energy of their people

• An "authoritarian lite" style of government—just enough central government to maintain control, defend the country, and direct infrastructure investment

The binding vision of economic growth is, very simply, wealth— not Marxism, not Maoism, not capitalism according to the American or European models, but a strong market that provides goods to individual consumers and profits to individual producers without much attention to democracy, social welfare, human rights, environmental degradations, or the massive overhead burden of an American-style legal system.

Corruption persists but does not obviate the massive profits. *Guanxi*—close connections and family networks—continues to cement relationships that facilitate business deal making. But at the higher levels of legitimate market activity, corruption is minimized by the fact that senior civil servants are now much better paid than they were.

Already by the turn of the century, China was experiencing the strains of two decades of 8–10 percent cumulative aggregate growth rates: strains on the infrastructure, environmental pollution, and speculative overhangs in financial markets that led to colossal bankruptcies here and there in the burgeoning economy. But the scale of the Chinese economy as a whole was large and diversified enough that its polycentric, decentralized, distributed structure kept the whole system from crashing, and indeed dampened down the colossal swings it had suffered through much of the 1980s and early 1990s, as it responded, whipcrack-style, to shifts in Beijing's political mood. Indeed, the most difficult part of this transformation for Beijing was allowing significant amounts of control to drop down to the local level, and providing a truly level playing field, so that even local officials had to pass power downward and not hoard it themselves. After Deng's death, the political philosophy had settled on a decentralized model that had many of the advantages of any network, the advantages that the Internet, for instance, has over a centrally switched architecture.

This image of an error-correcting communications system is more than a metaphor. China's use of computerized information technology, particularly satellite communications, is one of the key tools it has used to overcome one of its main problems: the tyranny of distance and the lack of adequate infrastructure. By leapfrogging expensive wireline solutions and moving straight to wireless satellite communications, China has bound hundreds of new cities and thousands of towns in distributed webs of transactions that take advantage of a legacy of village life and a lack of dependency on urban concentrations. China has become a land of forty Singapores, and 10,000 farm and factory villages with 40 million tiny enterprises, but no Mexico Cities, and no Rios—a networked economy.

Scenario One: China Web—The Dark Side

"It is the business of the future to be dangerous."
—*Alfred North Whitehead*

But what if it does not work? China tried once before to "leap forward" suddenly. In the Great Leap Forward, from 1958, China divided its vast rural population into communes, all responsible both for farming and for the building blocks of industry. Each village, for instance, was to build a "backyard" steel furnace. But the peasants knew little about steelmaking, or electric power production, or cement manufacturing. With millions of hands diverted from the fields into a commune system that gave no one any incentive to work, the back-breaking labor of growing rice and millet and pigs was not getting done. In 1958, a year of great weather, the harvest was good, but not nearly what it could have been. Peasants euphoric with the new system ate far more than they used to, even eating into next year's seed stocks. In 1959, nature was not so kind, combining flood and drought across China. By mid-year, people were slaughtering their breeding animals and their egg-laying chickens because they did not have enough to eat. Overzealous local officials in some areas melted down farm implements in order to meet the steel quotas. In 1960, the Soviets eventually withdrew all technical help. The leadership's flawed statistics, driven by the ideological enthusiasm of local officials, told them little of the looming disaster, so Beijing repeatedly increased the amount of food to be taken from the countryside to feed the cities, even as the famine deepened. In some areas, people even cannibalized the dead.

Across China, between 1959 and 1962, an estimated 20 to 30 million people died from famine due to the "Great Leap Forward." The lower figure would rival even the number of people killed in the Soviet Union in World War II, while the higher figure would be the largest number of people killed in any single country by any single cause in the history of the world.

It even approaches the lower estimates of the numbers of people killed worldwide during World War II, mankind's greatest-single disaster. It is as if someone made a mistake, and everyone in Canada starved to death.

Could this happen again? Probably not, if only because never again would China be so ideologically united, so driven to do whatever the party leaders say, whether it works or not.

Yet this scenario has its own dangers, and it too could become a "great leap backward." What if the attempt to leapfrog the industrial age never really gets off the ground? "Let them eat bytes" will not feed a billion peasants. What if China's new technological production cannot pay for food to make up for the lost agricultural production?

———————

Gujiang, Jiangxi Province, April 17, 2022

Two old men sit in the lantern light of a teashop on Gujiang's tiny square. It is a Sunday, their only evening for relaxation. They are grumpy at having to deal with this foreign researcher. After all, the one with the wispy beard says, "Why give so much attention to something that didn't work? Anyway, isn't it obvious what went wrong?"

At this the two men fall to squabbling. The translator keeps silent, waiting, apparently, for a victor to emerge. Finally the shorter of the two, clean-shaven, in a ragged blue sweater and knit skullcap, turns definitively to the foreigner and the translator and says: "It was the town chief and the council. After they assessed the whole town to build this fancy factory, they couldn't seem to pick the right products. They never got the road improved enough that the transport companies in Ji'an would send trucks up here. We had to take everything down there in private trucks or wagons."

"Besides," says his bearded friend. "I think they were putting most of the profits in their pockets.

"And hardly anybody was farming any more, since working in the factory paid better—but then the price of food went through the roof. You wouldn't believe it. So more people went back to farming. But you could only sell to the government, and they wouldn't raise the prices they paid to match the high prices people would pay for food. Of course, if you had the right *guanxi*, you could sell it on the sly and get away with it.

"By 2005, some people were actually starving, and the food riots started, people attacking the town and the central government food wholesale office, and the bank, with pitchforks and crowbars and rocks. They burned down the town chief's house. With him in it."

"What do you mean, 'they'?" says his bearded friend with a smile.

"Don't look at me, I wasn't there."

Across the square, the "Gujiang #1 Town Enterprise Factory" sign seems to be peeling slowly off the red bricks of the three-story building. The square itself seems to have become a dumping ground for building materials—piles of sand, bags of cement turned rock-hard in the weather, broken roof tiles. Power poles ring the square and they are frayed and broken. Where they hang to the ground, vines twine around them.

"But you still have the factory," says the researcher.

"Yes. We use it to store feed and rice."

Gujiang was emblematic of the problems that had erupted across China in the path of modernization. Now, after twenty-five years, almost all the experiments in the countryside have been abandoned, and rural China is what it always had been: a slow place with little money and barely enough food to keep the peasants alive and working.

The basic insight of Chinese leaders that led to the "Great Leap Forward" was correct: China's greatest potential lies in the labor surplus in the countryside. China uses few agricultural innovations, and the productivity of the peasants is very low. If that surplus labor could be put to use, China could rapidly build the world's strongest economy.

But the problems cropped up just as rapidly. Linking the towns by solar-powered wireless voice and data communications networks was relatively cheap and easy. With such a huge order, Motorola got the bid for telecomm kiosks below US$1,000 per unit and the cost of the handheld units below US$50. The hardest part turned out to be teaching hundreds of thousands of peasants (roughly a dozen per town) to use the data network for ordering, selling, and setting up national markets in goods and services.

But the transportation problem was not so easy to solve. Some towns concentrated on writing and debugging software, and they did not need transportation for their raw materials or finished goods. Everyone else still needed trucks and trains, and China was sadly deficient. In the mid-1990s, it had only one-third as many miles of railroads as the much smaller United States, one-third the tonnage of trucks, and one-sixth as many miles of roads (one-half as many kilometers as much-smaller India). Moreover, it turned out that even in simple assembly work, basic education made a difference, and the majority of the peasants were still illiterate.

But the deepest structural problems were right there in the villages, in the structure of village life. The people who made the decisions about the TVEs—where they would be built, how the money would be raised, what would be manufactured, who would be hired—were the same local elites, the local party chairmen and town councils, who had always run things. Their every incentive was to line their own pockets and those of their families and friends, and there were few legal or cultural checks on anything they wanted to do.

Under all these lay the basic problem, the same one that had always been there: There was no real labor surplus in the countryside. Chinese peasants were barely raising enough food for themselves and the burgeoning cities. Unless something drastic was done to raise their productivity, every hand taken away from the fields meant that much less food to eat. And nothing drastic was done, either by the government or by the villages. Everyone believed the vision: They would earn good hard cash and buy their food on the world market. But few villages made enough profit to support themselves, especially in the early years, and the demand from those that did drove up food prices around the world.

One more problem was just as fundamental: control. One reason why the Marshall Plan had succeeded so brilliantly in rescuing Europe from the wreckage of World War II is that the Americans provided capital, financial oversight, and expertise, but no control. They did not tell the Europeans how to rebuild. China was different. At every level, from Beijing to the village committee, Chinese officials could not bring themselves to let people lower down make real decisions about how to make money.

The result? Slow, plodding growth that did not even keep ahead of population growth. Everything else sacrificed for the need to simply grow enough rice.

"Are you concerned about your human rights, your economic rights?" the researcher asks.

The elder with the wispy beard smiles and shakes his head. "There is only one right in China," he says, "the right to be fed."

Scenario Spoilers

How to Turn the "China Web" Into a Disaster

We have seen these spoilers before. These are what brought Africa down. In turning Africa's bright post-colonial promise into today's rolling disaster, African leaders, Western governments, and global lenders employed every one of these methods in one way or another—and added tribal warfare facilitated by cheap, high-powered conventional weapons:

- Do not build the highways and railroads to get the raw materials to the countryside and the goods to market.

- Do not invest in healthcare, or in primary and secondary education. Channel your education investment into showcase universities.

- Loosen credit and ease bankruptcy laws. This will lower the penalty for foolish investment decisions and penalize savers.

- Ignore corruption and fraud.

- Give people incentives to abandon agriculture by keeping market prices low and penalizing agricultural innovations.

- Stick to personal rule (*renzhi*) and avoid the rule of law (*fazhi*).

- Make sure that village enterprises cannot hire outsiders, fire at will, set wages, or declare bankruptcy.

- At every level, interfere with the level below you, both with layers of rules and through arbitrary intervention.

- Design an ideal Town and Village Enterprise, and force everyone to copy that ideal model.

6

Scenario Two:
The New Mandarins

In this scenario, the powerful culture of kinship and connection (*guanxi*) becomes the matrix of the new China. This is a network scenario, like the first one. However, this is not a network formed around township and village enterprises (TVEs), but a network of networks whose nodes and threads are families, clans, village, and language groupings. There are perhaps fifty large familial (and faux-familial) nongeographic power structures twined, wound, interconnected, woven through thousands of enterprises across mainland China, through the arc of the Southeast Asian states, and reaching into the United States and Europe.

China loosens, but does not fragment. Beijing still rules. In fact, in many ways it is stronger, providing the legal framework and regulatory underpinnings that a rapidly maturing economy needs. But in most ways it is far weaker. It has gotten out of the business of regulating people's lives and thoughts. And if you want to know what's going on, or you want to start something, you don't ask the government ministries, you ask your cousin.

These fifty or so "tribes" include the language and village groups of the southeast coast (the Chiu Chao from Shantou, the Hakka from Meixian, and so on), Military Regions (MRs) and Military Districts (MDs) of the People's Liberation Army, the *taizi* ("princes and princesses," or sons and daughters) of the Party leadership, and "the class of '77." The Party itself has transformed from an instrument of deep social control to an instrument for making money—with a peculiar twist.

With the help of high-speed communications and transport—and the capital built up in the offshore Chinese community—these "tribes" become the equivalent of Japan's *keiretsu*, the vast networks of interlinked companies from manufacturers to banks to shipping firms, each connected to an old family name such as Mitsubishi, Honda, and Mitsui. Collectively, they come to wield a dominating influence, much like that of Japan's *Keidanren*, the "Federation of Economic Organizations" that for the forty years after 1945 was considered by many to be the true ruler of Japan.

Hierarchical and paternalistic, the top value of these "tribes" is loyalty; their great skills are speed and adaptability. They move into and out of opportunities with each shift of the wind, gambling with other people's money, taking their cut, keeping most of their own money safely offshore. The heads of these "tribes"—the new Mandarins—are the real powers in China. As China grows, they increasingly become major players on the global stage.

Xiamen, Fujian Province, June 21, 2022

"Old Wu, the guests are arriving." It was the new maid, whose name he did not know. Wu Yuejin just grunted in reply. He would take a few more moments alone out here on the balcony. He had made his bows and lit the incense at the little outdoor shrine of Guan Di, the god of war. Now he just wanted to watch the sunset. Wu was not usually given to nostalgia. He was a practical man, no cloud-headed poet. Still, tonight was his birthday. Friends and family were gathering. He leaned on the carved and lacquered rail, smoking. In his black silk jacket, his black hair in a fashionable new "Hainan" cut, the wide, round man looked about fifty. He was seventy.

He loved summer sunsets in Xiamen, when the falling sun flashed straight down the bay from distant Zhangzhou. In his eyes, it was even more beautiful now than when he was young. He remembered rice terraces, villages, fishing junks. Now from Xinglin and Jimei to the north all the way around to Longhai and Haicheng, the bay's edge was a curtain wall of glass, steel, and concrete: offices, factories, container ports, warehouses. From this angle, twenty-seven stories up in the penthouse of his favorite building, the sunlight seemed to slash red-brown through the smog, glinting off the highrises and speckling the water in the marina at the base of the building. To him, the scene looked like struggle, it looked like years of work, and it looked like money.

It was all Hokkien. A lot of actual capital that built it was foreign, of course. Why use your own money when you can use someone else's? But from where he sat he could point to and name the buildings he had financed, the projects he had built—and he could tell you the names of the people that he had put in charge of each one, all of them from Xinxu, his father's home village, his *laojia*.

Wu Yuejin's grandfather, a modest landowner, had been killed in the land reforms, and his great uncles were forced to become "muddy shanks" rice farmers. Wu Yuejin's father, Wu Guang, and his uncles fled Xinxu. Wu Yuejin grew up in Taiwan, knowing of uncles and cousins in San Francisco, Manila, and Jakarta—and third and fourth cousins in Xiamen and elsewhere in Fujian.

They did not think of themselves, particularly, as being Chinese. Everyone was Chinese. Being Chinese did not mean anything less abstract than, say, being a human. Rather, they thought of themselves as people from Xinxu, and second as people from Hokkien.

Wu Guang had always been in one business or another— property, a small restaurant, part ownership in a factory that made toys for the American market. The family financed their businesses the old-fashioned way, through the *hui*, or the credit club. Their family and a few others from Xinxu and nearby villages would pool part of their savings. When they met each month, the chairman would dole out loans through a simple auction system—whoever in the club bid the highest interest would get the money.

Or they might simply go to a wealthy person in their family or their name-and-place association and ask for a loan. There would be no interest on this loan, only *guanxi*: Someday the wealthy man might need to ask a favor. Would you repay the loan? Of course. If you did not, you would lose face—and face is worth more than any amount of money or any labor that it took to get the money. Sometimes they took part in bigger enterprises. For this, they would join a *kongsi*, a kind of corporation in which people—always people from the same *laojia*, or the next one down the road—would pool their money for some specific enterprise (to build a factory, for example) and have voting rights in major decisions.

By the time Deng Xiaoping had set up the Special Enterprise Zones in the 1980s, Wu Guang had already been sneaking back into China on a regular basis, bringing little gifts of cash in the traditional red envelopes to friends and relations in Xinxu and Xiamen itself, financing hidden businesses, cultivating *guanxi*. By then Wu Yuejin had a degree in engineering from the University of California, and he had joined his father in the family business.

While in California, Wu Yuejin had been exposed to many cultural influences that had broadened his understanding. But one struck him more profoundly than all others and stayed with him, not because it changed him, but because it helped him see. It was as if he were a fish who had suddenly been given an understanding of water. This influence was a Hollywood film about a family from southern Italy now living in New York. It was called *The Godfather*. There was a novel, and eventually two sequels came out, all of which he brought back to Taiwan with him. It struck him that families from southern Italy were much like families from southern China, and the ties of blood, of name, of village, were much the same. He felt he understood the Corleones implicitly, especially the young Don Michael.

In the 1980s, based on the *guanxi* Wu Guang had built up, they went into business on the mainland in a big way. It was so cheap there, and people were so eager to work. Wu Guang's brothers, other *laojia* contacts, and people they knew through their contacts in Singapore, Jakarta, Vancouver, San Francisco, and New York acted as funnels for foreign investment money. Foreign partners were falling all over themselves to invest. You did not even have to sell them on the concept. They had a gold-rush fever about China, the money came leaping from their hands.

Wu Yuejin learned quickly. His father was literate and unusually learned, at least in one book: Sunzi's *Art of War*, which he loved to quote. Wu Guang told him, "As Master Sun would say, the money 'can be likened to the cascading of pent-up waters thundering through a steep gorge.'"

In this fashion father and son built a CD factory, a bicycle factory, an apartment building—the growth was so fast it was hard to keep track of. Soon there was no one left in Xinxu who was not working for them. This was the hardest part, actually. The Wus never wanted to hire someone they did not trust, and how could you trust someone who was not from your village, much less someone who did not even speak Hokkien?

But the foreigners—oh, they were so easy. You could get an American partner in some development project, an office building, for example. They would put up most of the money and leave control to the Wus. After all, what did they know of managing a project in China? Then the Wus would come back to the partner for more money: There was an official they had to bribe. There was a special sewage fee that had to be paid. The people who were renting rooms in the building they were going to tear down would have to be compensated. When they had squeezed the project as dry as they could, they would sell their minority interest to some other foreigner and take back a management fee indexed to inflation. The profits were huge. His uncles used the Mandarin phrase *zai lao wai*— "Slaughter the foreigner." Wu Guang preferred to quote Master Sun: "At first be like a modest maiden, and the enemy will open his door; afterward be as swift as a scurrying rabbit, and the enemy will be too late to resist you."

By the 1990s, Wu Guang was leaving more and more of the business to his son. Wu Guang was in his seventies and frail. He had been overjoyed by the discovery and publication of the Yingueshan texts of Master Sun, and he spent much of his time studying them. Wu Yuejin, for his part, had mastered other books, and he took the business in a new direction. At Berkeley, he had studied American history, which included the story of the building of the great railroads. They were financed in an intriguing fashion: The entrepreneur would provide a public good—a railroad—and take his profit not so much from the freight tariffs as from the development rights to the land along the way. Wu saw that he could do this in Fujian. Now in his forties, he applied the idea over and over in his father's homeland, building highways (for the development rights at the junctions and a guaranteed portion of the tolls), bridges (for the rights on both ends), ports (for the rights around the port, and the freight-handling concessions), railroads, and light-rail systems. He always built with other people's money, took a cut, kept the rights if he could, and tied the foreigners' return to the riskiest part—the tolls, for instance, which the provincial government could change any time. He never invested the family's own money deeply in Fujian, except for Xinxu, which had become a model town, with clean sidewalks, good lighting, elegant shops, a park, and a beautiful graveyard where he buried his father next to his grandfather in 1997. No, except for what he needed as seed money for new Fujian projects, Wu kept the family's own money invested in Taiwan, the United States, or Switzerland. There was always an escape hatch. The keys, in fact, were flexibility, swiftness, adaptability. As his father used to quote Master Sun: "There is no invariable strategic advantage (shi) or invariable position (xing) that can be relied on at all times."

As early as 2003, Wu Yuejin's name had begun appearing on lists of the world's dollar billionaires. He always found those lists amusing, since their estimates of his wealth usually ran from one-tenth to one-quarter of his family's actual worth.

Wu Yuejin threw the stub of his cigarette off into the dusk and stirred from the railing. At the shrine, he lit one more stick of incense and stuck it in the sand bowl before the stern and furious lacquered image of Guan Di, and he went inside.

First there was the reception here in his penthouse, then later a great banquet on a barge in the bay. At the reception, all were Hokkien. In fact, most were family: his son Clinton Wu, his American cousins Darryl and Marlie Woo and Randall Wu-Levy, his one surviving uncle Wu Kuo-feng, from Jakarta—in all, about thirty of his family and his closest friends and contacts.

When the party moved to the boat, it changed its character. Clinton had chartered the largest floating restaurant in the bay (a onetime Taiwanese Navy buoy tender) and invited more than 500 people. Old Wu joked, "I hope it doesn't sink, or China will be in chaos."

The 500 people on the boat were not just friends. They were leaders, like himself and his children, of the groups that ran China—and every handshake triggered a memory. For instance, taking the breeze in the bow of the old ship, Wu Yuejin found Harry Tian, of the Taishan Cantonese, Ren Yiren the Hakka leader, and Lin Dagui of the Chiu Chao, his partners in his first foray into politics. In 2001, things had come to a head in the Hong Kong Special Administrative Region (SAR). Beijing was pouring troops and tanks into the former colony and preparing to declare martial law over some demonstrations about freedom of speech and religion that Wu thought stupid and pointless. He had put together a committee to go and explain things to the party leadership in Beijing: himself, Tian, Ren, and Lin. They had brought in General Zhu Shunzhang (since 1990 the PLA had invested hundreds of millions into the heated Hong Kong economy), and Deng Zhifang, Deng Xiaoping's youngest son (to represent the *taizi*, the children of China's leaders of the 1980s and 1990s). Deng had approached his long-time business partner, Hong Kong billionaire Li Ka-shing, and Li had joined them. Wu had his personal 757 pick them all up, and together they flew to Beijing. They had no trouble getting an audience with the top leadership—between them they had plenty of *guanxi* for that. They had laid out in detail just what it would cost China—and the leaders personally—to shut down Hong Kong's vibrant, noisy, messy culture in pursuit of political neatness. It was not about free speech. It was about Beijing's itch for over-control. They were harassing the Catholic Church, which ran most of the schools, clinics, and hospitals in the SAR with remarkable discipline and efficiency. They were censoring the film industry, which used to be second only to the United States and India, until there was hardly anything left of it. They were demanding full records from the precious metals exchange—when the lack of records was precisely the factor that made it the most popular exchange in the world. The list went on and on. The message was, "You're killing the goose that laid the golden egg."

The second message was a face-saving way to back down, a method that involved a lot of harrumphing about foreign instigators, the arrest of a few expendable people, and loud declarations of socialist values, along with a stand-down order to all the troops, followed over weeks and months by a quiet loosening of controls, so that capitalism and efficiency could get back on track.

It worked. Wu thought afterward that it was not so much the information they brought—presumably the leadership had heard these arguments and knew these facts. It was who had brought the facts, and the enormous wealth, power, and *guanxi* they represented.

They had not stopped there. Wu had put together or been part of other ad-hoc groups over the years. In the early 2000s, they had begun voicing their concerns about appointments in the coast provinces, from governors and judges to mayors, until it became a matter of course for the Party to pass appointments by the Elders (as he and his peers came to be known). More often than not, the Elders suggested appointees to the Party, and the Party rarely dared to turn down the suggestion. Wu knew, through his informal contacts, that this eventually came to be the situation all over China. Elders could call off investigations, get land decisions cleared, have the right people appointed. They could get things done, and the Party acted as their secretariat and mouthpiece.

By 2007, he was ready to take on the other big festering question, Taiwan. It was another issue he thought "stupid." The argument was supposedly ideological, but in fact the only real ideology left on either side was about who controlled what. Wu was able to broker an agreement that finessed the problem. Taiwan acknowledged Beijing's sovereignty and joined Fujian in a new Special Administrative Region with its own elected government and a militia made of units of the ROC forces and the PLA Military Region. Wu and other Elders put enough pressure on the Party that it found ways to adjust the agreement, in the details about appointments, taxes, and who controlled the police, to assure the Taiwanese that they could continue their freewheeling political and social culture. He was proud of that, more proud than of anything he had ever done—and here, standing by a fat black stanchion on the port rail watching the lights of Xiamen come on, was the governor of the Taiwan-Fujian SAR, Dick Chan.

"Old Chan, so glad you could come."

"Old Wu, how could I not celebrate your great and venerable age? Congratulations. It is a beautiful party."

"All that I could scrape together. I hope that our meager fare and accommodations will do."

As he became more powerful, Wu felt something else kick in, some deep Confucian remnant that made him look to broader responsibilities than just adding to his own family fortune and protecting his position. He and his fellow Elders had begun to push the Party and the government to build strong environmental rules into law, and to professionalize the judiciary and make it more independent. This raised the price of buying judges, and kept bought justice in the hands of people like himself. For everybody else, it provided a semblance of a "level playing field," which foreign investors liked.

So the Party steadily lost power, pulling back its tentacles from the neighborhoods and villages, as the Elders repeatedly explained to the Party what was good for business and what was bad. Yet the Party had gone through perhaps the most interesting shift of all. In the beginning, it had a powerful ideological *raison d'etre* built on the real needs of the people. After the Great Leap Forward, the communes, the Cultural Revolution, and then Deng's revolution, there were only two reasons left to be in the Party: It gave you lots of power over other people, and it gave you the *guanxi* to make money, if you had the personal ability to do it.

As the Party pulled back from its micromanagement of people's lives, it became frail. It desperately needed some new way to keep the loyalty of its 60 million members. Jiang Dechang, a grandson of Jiang Zemin, was the genius who came up with the model that rescued the Party—and it was the horse that Jiang rode to the chairmanship of the Party.

Jiang reasoned: As it eased its hold on social control, the main thing the Party had left was a network of special connections that allowed members to make money. But not everyone in the Party had access to the right kind of deals. It still was not that easy. Why not take advantage of the Party's nationwide people-to-people network? The Party would endorse certain products, the kinds of things everybody buys, from soap to tires to film. The local Party cadres would sell these in their area. The prices would be very competitive, since with all that volume the Party could get very good prices from the manufacturers. The Party would set up a fulfillment operation, so the local cadres did not have to deal with warehousing and shipping and such. The local cadres would get a cut, and so would every level of the Party above them, right back to Beijing. Any level could use some of the money they received to promote the products any way they liked—advertising, sponsoring concerts or sports teams, anything. Any Party member who recruited a new member would get a piece of the new member's sales.

It was beautiful. The people would get products they needed at better, more efficient prices, everybody in the Party would get rich, and the Party's image would be rehabilitated from petty nosy dictator to creator of wealth.

Wu remembered the first time Jiang had pitched the idea to him. Jiang was making the rounds of the Elders to gather backing for the shift. They had met in his board room with its giant teak table and its view of the dockyards. Jiang had given a full presentation, with charts and graphs thrown up on the screen from his foldaway computer.

Wu had broken out laughing, "You're trying to turn the Communist Party of China into a multilevel marketing scheme? I've seen this before. When I was in college in the States, there were all these people into network marketing, selling telephone services, cosmetics, natural foods, soaps, and detergents. Some of them were making piles of money. They were always asking me to join them. But here? In the Communist Party?"

Jiang seemed horrified. "No, Old Wu, pardon my effrontery, but you do not understand at all. Obviously my poor presentation was not clear enough. This so-called network marketing, or multilevel marketing, as you call it, is the worst of the scum thrown up by the putrefaction of Western capitalism. It is no more than what they call in the United States a 'Ponzi scheme,' in which money flows from the new recruits to the veterans, impoverishing those who joined too late. No, my 'Dynamic Socialism' is the next stage of the glorious thought of Chairman Mao and theory of our supreme leader Deng, following Deng's shining promise to break the bonds of class. Mao scientifically analyzed the contradictions in socialist society, profoundly illustrated the laws of class struggle, and put forth the necessary theory for the continuation of the revolution. Old Deng showed that if socialism is to triumph, it must shift its tactics, as Chairman Mao did in the Long March. We must heed the precious words of Mao and Deng to raise the level of the people, strengthen the Party, and transform the fatherland by bringing wealth within the reach of every class."

This was Jiang's final genius: He wrapped his plan in the rhetoric of socialism and in the twin auras of Mao and Deng. It caught on like wildfire in the demoralized Party, especially when cadres actually began making good money at it. The Party had gone from being a hated social control mechanism to being the money machine of the masses, and new members flocked to it.

Wu saw Chairman Jiang coming toward him across the deck of the old ship and called out, "Old Jiang, I am so honored that you could come to the birthday party of such a humble person as myself."

"Old Wu, it is Elders like you who have rebuilt China. May you live to a great age! All praise to Comrade Deng and the socialist road to wealth! Happy birthday!"

Scenario 2: The New Mandarins—The Dark Side

"Things Fall Apart, the Center Cannot Hold"

Where "The New Mandarins" represents a relatively benign scenario following from the rule of fifty families, the following scenario shows how such cronyism could turn sour.

Xiamen, Fujian Province, June 21, 2022:

"Old Wu, the guests are arriving." It was the new maid, whose name he did not know.

"Guests? What guests?"

The maid stood with her head bowed just outside the door to the penthouse balcony. "It is your glorious birthday, Old Wu. Some of your friends insisted on coming to greet you on this most auspicious occasion."

Wu Yuejin grunted, then turned back to the sunset. "I will take a few more moments out here on the deck." He had made his bows and lit the incense at the little outdoor shrine of Guan Di, the god of war. Now he just wanted to watch the sunset.

The sun was disappearing in angry gold-red bars into the smoke of distant Zhangzhou. He wondered how much of it was gone by now. The guns had been growling all day, and as the dusk came on he could see the brilliant purple flashes of laser cannons as close as Xinglin and Jimei and the orange flames that engulfed their targets. Most of Jimei seemed to be a firestorm. The smoke obliterated most of the bay to the north. This far away, Wu could still smell the burning—it had the pungency of smoldering rubber, chemicals, fuel, and explosives. It made his eyes water, and he dabbed at them with his sleeve. Oddly, it was even more disturbing to hear small-arms fire from the streets below, the roar of automatic weapons, the crack-crack of pistols. Wu Yuejin was seventy, and he was tired.

His gut churned to see foreigners—Hakka and Chiu Chao, especially—destroying so much that the Hokkien had built. They were all units of the PLA, of course, but he knew the units involved, their commanders, and their men. They were not Hokkien. They were outsiders. Two days before, Xinxu had been overrun, and the sketchy reports he had received gave a picture of unmitigated savagery.

It had started so well. They thought they had resolved the Hong Kong mess in 2001, and pretty soon they had all the influence they needed. But at the same time things became more and more difficult. After some good starts in the 1990s, the law began to just fall apart after the turn of the millennium. There was no court you could not buy, no agency ruling that was not available for a price. Just to keep foreign investors involved, Wu and his fellow Elders had tried to work out between them an alternative court system with its own Enforcers to keep the peace and help maintain commercial statutes in their own areas. But it could never work, because the families did not trust each other. Of course, how could you trust these people? Look where they came from.

And the rot at the core could not be stopped. By 2005, the Communist Party had broken into factions, full of revolutionary rhetoric as always, but in reality just scrambling for power, each faction representing one group or another—the Hakka, the Shanghainese, the *taizidang* (or the "princes" faction), the Sichuanese, the Taishan, and all the little family groups within each of these. The fight shifted from one group to another behind the scenes, with families even switching sides and allying with people from another region if they thought it would help their own clan. But for years on end, no single group was strong enough to eliminate the others and take charge.

Without this backbone, the central government was more and more ignored by the provincial governments, the regional branches of the People's Bank of China, educational institutions, and law enforcement officers. Its ability to collect taxes, weakened in the reforms of the 1980s, never recovered, and it went into a tailspin after 2006. Their attempts to slowly wean the state-owned enterprises from the teat of the central state had turned into abrupt cut-offs, with nearly 80 million workers not only laid off, but deprived of housing, education, and medical care, all in 2007 and 2008.

In the big inflation scare of 2010, the People's Bank and the Beijing government were clearly too weak to do anything, so a consortium of banks from Hong Kong and the southern provinces stepped in to stabilize the situation. The Hong Kong dollar became the de facto currency of Guangdong and Fujian. A group of Shanghai banks issued currency that was recognized in Jiangsu, Zhejiang, and Anhui. Sichuan followed suit, and soon there were dozens of currencies around the country, some backed by a whole province, some just by a single, family-controlled bank. Some provinces set up customs units at the border to shake down shippers for duties. This was all very bad for business.

After the failure of the Zhongnanhai Putsch in 2015, the Beijing government ceased to function except as keeper of the National Archives, the museums and universities that accrue to a national capital. There was a president and a full set of ministers, but they did not even try to issue any directives. They only bothered with the offices because you could still use a national ministry to make money.

The only thing that held the country together was the People's Liberation Army—not only the fact that it still existed, but that it had its own sources of funds, that it had a full array of tactical and strategic nuclear weapons and the means to deliver them, and that it commanded several million peasant soldiers willing to take their tanks and machine guns wherever their commanders told them to go, and shoot when their commanders said to shoot.

The leaders of the PLA let it be known, loudly and often, that they had one goal: national unity. You could quibble about ideology, you could ignore the Beijing government, but if you tried to declare independence, you were as good as dead. They were as interested in making money as anyone else, but they were nationalist to the bone.

That was fine. What good was having your own country when you could do all you wanted to anyway—without any of a government's responsibility for the environment and international treaties? Besides, the Elders, the provincial governors, the governor of the Bank of Hong Kong, everyone in a position to declare independence had all read the detailed reports of what actually happened in Tiananmen Square and for miles around it in June 1989. Any army that was willing to machine-gun unarmed crowds of its own citizens repeatedly for days on end had to be respected. Whenever the PLA made nationalist noises, they and other luminaries all loudly proclaimed their devotion to the Chinese nation and the PLA as the guarantor of national peace and integrity.

In private, though, the families, the *taizidang*, and all the other factions hated the PLA because it was such a powerful counterforce.

They were ceaseless in their efforts to obligate this unit or that commander to them through favors, investment opportunities, or ties of blood and marriage.

This perpetual tugging and seduction had its affect. The PLA was far from united. It had always been controlled, through the Military Affairs Commission and the Ministry of Defense, by the Party and the government—now both vacant, powerless shells driven by the feuds among the warring families. The last person to single handedly control that vast force had been Deng Xiaoping. In order to keep things on an even keel, the PLA had established a committee, with members of the General Staff, the General Rear Services Department, the Navy Department, and the Air Force Department, that it named the High Command. But no single strong figure emerged to be the voice and face of the PLA.

Then, in 2019, all hell broke loose. Hong Kong had elected its own legislature for years—a noisy, fractious, entertaining bunch with no real power. Like all the provinces, the Hong Kong SAR had a governor appointed by Beijing—though in reality, he or she was picked by the Elders of the five families that ruled there and then approved by the PLA. Now the Hong Kong legislature passed a law declaring that the people would elect their own governor. The SAR governor refused to sign it. The legislature declared it law anyway and set a date for the election—June 4, 2019, the thirtieth anniversary of the Tiananmen Square Massacre.

Many in the PLA thought this was a direct slap at them. The High Command issued a declaration that a direct election would be tantamount to declaring independence, and that it would not be allowed. But the commander of the Guangzhou Military Region, General Wei Yi, took a further step, apparently without consulting his colleagues. General Wei, here in the land of the Taishan and the polyglot riff-raff of Hong Kong, had ties to the Hakka and the Chiu Chao.

He declared Hong Kong to be in insurrection and crossed the border at Shenzhen with four infantry divisions, accompanied by tanks and armored personnel carriers. He declared that he would depose the legislature and prevent the election. All through the New Territories, at Tsuen Wan, at Kwun Tong, at Kowloon, crowds of people flooded onto bridges and intersections, and Wei's troops fired on them, in scenes vividly reminiscent of those thirty years before.

Old Wu had been very agitated. This could not be allowed to happen, or everything the Wus and the Hokkien had built would be gone. He called in every chit he had. He had tremendous *guanxi* with the High Command. Some of them were distant cousins of his, others were in-laws, others silent investors.

Wei was determined to occupy Hong Kong itself, but before he could get to the island, saboteurs blew up the bridges. He could not get to the island now without help. A number of members of the High Command had deep personal and financial ties to Hong Kong, not least of them Admiral Li Minzhu, head of the Navy Department, the husband of Wu's niece. Ships appeared off Kowloon, but they made no effort to help Wei. In fact, after some tense exchanges with Beijing, Wei saw the naval task force reposition itself, with its guns trained on his divisions massed along the Kowloon docks. Wei radioed to the Navy that he would blow them out of the water if they did not stand down. He got no reply. He ordered a machine gunner on a nearby tank to take aim at the bridge of the nearest ship, a light cruiser, and fire. The cruiser replied with five-inch guns, demolishing a row of twelve tanks. Suddenly there was a war, something China had not seen within its borders for nearly seventy years.

The Fuzhou Military Region came in on the Navy's side, but the Air Force backed General Wei. General Tian, the Fuzhou commander, was Hokchiu, and most of his men were Hokkien. Ren Yiren, the Hakka leader, and Lin Dagui of the Chiu Chao backed General Wei as well, putting the enormous financial resources of their families at his disposal. When five of General Tian's six divisions were pinned down near Shantou, Tian sent a secret call for help to the Taiwan government. They answered, in a move that caught everyone by surprise. Taiwan landed troops near Chaoyang and caught Wei in a pincer movement.

The war spread rapidly beyond the southern coast as factions lined up, changed sides, maneuvered for advantage, seceded, rejoined. Everyone, on all sides, thought the bloodshed would be short. Modern wars are too bloody to last long. But this one had lasted three years now, see-sawing back and forth. There was no way to tell how many had been killed. Some authorities said 7 million, some said 12 million. The first nuclear exchange occurred on the Shanxi-Shaanxi border, tacticals let off by a panicky general caught with his back to the Yellow River and his flank on the Great Wall. He seemed to think that if he blew down several hundred yards of the Wall he could create an escape hatch for his troops, but the piles of rubble were as hard to get over as the Wall had been. There had been half a dozen other nuclear exchanges since then. Bridges, dams, infantry divisions, even one suburb of Wuhan had disappeared under radioactive mushroom clouds.

What was so sad, to Old Wu, was that after three years of this devastation, China was no closer to unification—and China was ruined. There was no business except supplying the troops. Most of the infrastructure he and the other Elders had built had been destroyed. Tian, Wei, and a half-dozen other generals had become virtual warlords, with their own governments.

Old Wu sighed. The harbor was dark by now. A Taiwanese ship, a tender of some kind, was incongruously parked at the marina below the building. He turned and looked inside. The apartment was full of people, but he could not make them out in the failing light. He lit one more stick of incense and went inside.

As he shut the door, he saw that they were soldiers. His servants were nowhere to be seen. An officer stepped forward, a stern young man with the brim of his cap pulled down nearly to his dark glasses. "Old Wu," said the officer. "General Tian sends his respects. He said to tell his godfather that it is time to leave."

"Tell him he should not worry about me. I am just an old man."

"Sorry, venerable Wu. We are losing Xiamen. He ordered me not to leave without you. He sent a small ship to take you away to Taiwan. It is waiting."

Wu sighed. "All right. Would you get my jacket, please? It's in the closet by the front door. And the suitcase under it. It's packed."

"You were going on a trip?" said the officer.

"No. No, I've always kept a bag packed. For thirty-five years. 'Things fall apart, the center cannot hold. Mere anarchy is loosed' Never mind. Let's go."

Scenario Spoilers

How to Turn the "The New Mandarins" Into a Disaster

- Stick to personal rule (*renzhi*) and avoid the rule of law (*fazhi*).

- Ignore corruption and fraud.

- Do not build any vision of China's future beyond the scramble for money.

- Leave the PLA without a strong master by failing to create any new vision for China's Communist Party beyond the scramble for money and power.

- Avoid constitutional changes that would regularize succession.

- Starve the central government of taxes and authority.

- Delay rationalizing the state-owned enterprises.

- Make no attempt to woo the PLA into global efforts to decrease tactical and strategic nuclear stocks.

7

Scenario Three:
The Thief of Beijing

"[Foreign conspirators] support and buy over so-
called dissidents through whom they foster blind worship of the Western world and propagate the political
patterns, sense of values, decadent traits, and lifestyle
of the Western capitalist world."
                    —Jiang Zemin, General Secretary of the Communist
                              Party of China, September 29, 1989

"I can't stand people with a sense of mission."
—Wang Shuo, television writer, 1992, to Orville Schell,
                        author of Mandate of Heaven: The Legacy of
                        Tiananmen Square and the Next Generation of
                                                    China's Leaders.

In this scenario, China collapses into a morass of decadence, corruption, and greed. With 100 million robber barons clawing for
wealth at any cost, China's environment becomes a sewer of dam-
age and waste. The few shreds of old values that survived Maoism
and the Cultural Revolution dissolve under the acid of atavistic
competition for money, status, and power.

But finally the lawlessness and environmental chaos begin to
choke the system that fed it. It gets harder and harder to make
real money—and harder to live a decent life, no matter how much

money you have. The elite—billionaires, gangsters, government ministers, Party officials, and *taizi*—slide deeper and deeper into a fear of chaos. Even those who had hated the old Maoist repression realize that they need order, and they need it fast. They find a savior, someone who can give them order—a charismatic military leader. With backing in all the right quarters, he is able to put down rebellions and unite the country, and then ruthlessly expunge all "parasites on the social order," from judges on the take to pornographers, from polluters to rock stars. But he quickly establishes the new order: China as the world's largest kleptocracy, and himself as chief plunderer.

Beidaihe, Hebei Province, June 21, 2022

Summer had come to Beidaihe with a grandmother's gentleness, the way it always had in Liao Lihua's memory. There must have been summer storms at some point in those sixty-three years, but this is how she remembered Beidaihe summers: mild, the surf roaring in the distance, the gentle arc of the white beaches, the blue of the sea, the red tile roofs peeking through the lush growth of pine and cypress, the secluded paths and artful, winding footbridges. To her, Beidaihe meant flowers: chrysanthemums, orchids, roses. It meant the wide green lawns of the estates of the party leaders and the ministries, and the snap that salt air gives to a breeze coming off the sea. She remembers more than once capping an uproarious night by taking the man to Yingjiaoting, the Eagle Horn Pavilion on the clifftop north of town, to watch the first rays of the sun dance across the sea toward them—a great tonic after a night of indulgence.

She was a "Party girl." She remembered years ago talking to a young American researcher, not unlike this earnest young *New York Times* reporter sitting in front of her now. She had explained what she did, and that is what he had said they would call her in the States. They had other words for it, but that was a nice way of putting it. She had told him that she knew or could guess exactly what the not-so-nice words translated into, thank you, and they were not appropriate words for the work she did. She kept the best house in Beidaihe; in fact, she dared him to find a finer one in all China. Only the finest, best-looking, most talented young women worked for her, and her customers were from the elite, none of the riff-raff, no matter how much money they had—they had to have references.

Then the reporter had told her the pun in the term, the several meanings of the word "party" in English, and she had thought it even more appropriate. For all these years, many of her best customers, and her staunchest protectors in times of need, had been stalwarts of the Party.

"Yes, Grandma Liao," said the reporter, using the respectful honorific for an older woman, "though I have not availed myself of its services, it is certainly a most beautiful house."

She sniffed in polite offense at the thought that a mere reporter might be able to become a customer in her house. An American, at that. Though he did have remarkably good Mandarin for an American. They were sitting over tea at a small table next to an indoor pool. Beyond the glass spread broad lawns and the dark green forest. The lawns fell away, revealing the view to the sea far below. With enough imagination one could almost see Manchuria or Shandong in the distance.

"Taste the water," she said.

"The pool water, Grandma?"

She nodded. He leaned over and dipped a teaspoon in the pool.

"It's sea water, Grandma!"

She nodded primly once more. "Pumped almost two kilometers up from the ocean. Fresh. Changed every day." She laughed. "I can see it on your face. You are thinking, what an extravagance for an old Party girl. But it was not my extravagance. It was the extravagance of a Party man. This house, with its twenty-five rooms and its sea water pool, was built a half-century ago by a minister of defense named Lin Biao."

"Did he name it 'Hotel California'?"

"Oh, no, I did. Several of my clients said that the sea and the hills reminded them of California. And there was an old song of that name, have you ever heard it?"

"Oh, yes, 'Hotel California,' by the Eagles. It's an old standard. My grandfather loves their music. They play it all the time on the speakers in the old folk's homes these days." He paused and studied his notes. "May I ask how you came to be . . . in business for yourself, Grandma?"

"Well, you see, I was raised here in Beidaihe, at least in the summers, and in the winters in Zhongnanhai, the compound of the Party leaders in Beijing. My father was a very important man in the Party, sometimes a deputy assistant minister, sometimes on special commissions. But the Cultural Revolution left me mother-less and fatherless. All I had left were my connections to the big Party leaders. I needed protection. So at sixteen, I became the mis-tress of a man I had known as 'Uncle Zhu,' a vice minister. I had apartments here and in Beijing, on the Avenue of Eternal Peace. I had a huge allowance, and I wore beautiful clothes—imagine, Mao was still alive, and everyone was wearing those horrid little suits. When I turned twenty-one, I could tell he was tiring of me, so I talked to him about my situation. He told me that many of his friends had admired me. He said that if I allowed them to come visit me from time to time, they would pay well. My friend told me there was a big market for the right kind of woman at the high end, a classy woman like the women in Paris or Hollywood.

"I was humiliated. I thought I was too good for that sort of thing. But I recovered quickly. Besides, what else could I do? In a few days, I told him to go ahead and contact his friends.

"I did good business. It kept me in high style, nice clothes, a beau-tiful apartment, much better than the ordinary people. And I got to know all the best people—I would only see the very best, and besides, my prices were very high. In the late 1980s, before all the turmoil in Tiananmen Square, a customer who was a general, on the General

Staff, in fact, had a suggestion. He said the PLA was looking for investment opportunities. He said if I were to set up a very exclusive house, they might be willing to invest on good terms.

"It was a great opportunity. It took me a year to find a good place right near Zhongnanhai, to use my *guanxi* to get hold of the place, get all the right permits, and refurbish it—I have always had big *guanxi*—and to find the right young women, to train them, buy them good clothes, teach them how to do make-up so they looked elegant and not trashy.

"Just as I opened, the turmoil happened. On June 4, there was shooting right on my street, people killed! It was horrible. And I had almost no business for months afterward. If it had not been for my investors standing by me, I would have gone bankrupt.

"The one good thing that came out of it was that one of the pro-testers came to me looking for a place to hide out. She wasn't on the most-wanted list or anything, but she was still afraid. I gave her a place to stay and hired her to answer the phones. Six months later, after she came to understand how much money the girls were mak-ing, she said she wanted to do more than answer phones. She was one of the best. Made a lot of money, and eventually opened her own house.

"That's what the 1990s were about. When I started, it was hard to find women to do this work. They thought it shameful. And they would have no official work unit—it was risky. But in the 1990s, especially after Deng made his *nanxun*, his southern journey, in 1992, everyone was out to make money. I was flooded with young women who wanted to work for me—many of them beautiful, edu-cated, with good recommendations. They just wanted to make money as fast as possible.

"You see, getting paid for being with the men was only the beginning. The other part was being able to invest in all the things the men told us. That was the real money.

"The 1990s were a wild time. Everything was money, money, money. The government and the Party lost control of the culture.

Every type of book and video was coming out. If you couldn't publish it in the 'red' channel, with the official approval number, in the official stores, you could publish it in the 'white' channel, with a private publisher, who would just buy the official approval. The government couldn't ban the practice, because the main way the official publishers made any money was by selling the approvals. And if the government just banned something outright, it would show up a few days later in the street stalls—the 'black' channel—for three times the price, selling three times as well.

"The cities were not what they used to be. They were suddenly full of neon, and money changers, and street girls, and karaoke bars, and big stores. Everybody was selling everything. A lot of cities, including Shanghai, even sold their city halls.

"Rock music just got out of control. There was this fellow Cui Jian in the 1980s. And then Hou Dejian. And in the 1990s, Zhang Chu, with his *Red Rock and Roll* making fun of the old Party songs. And videos. Everybody got satellite dishes and could watch anything they wanted. The news stands were full of trashy tabloids. The young people called themselves *liumang*—outlaws, gangsters—and it was true, that's all they were.

"In my own business, I realized that suddenly I had a lot of competition. There were houses everywhere—some of them even sponsored by the PLA and the Public Security Bureau. I visited Shanghai in 1995. The PLA had a house called the Casablanca at the Rainbow Hotel on Yan'an Road—it had karaoke in every room. And the PSB had two—the Shanghai Moon Club on Zhaojiabang Road, very nice, and the Protect the Secret Club on Huashan Road. In order to compete, I had to get even better. I had to offer what no one else could, not full of strobe lights and karaoke and strippers and people doing private things in public. No, my house had the very finest women, the best food, special services for whatever taste, all in complete privacy, with the very greatest discretion.

"There still seemed to be a market for quality. I survived, and did well. In fact, a lot of these new *kuanye*—cash gods—became my customers, the *geti hu*—entrepreneurs—and the *dahu*—big players in the stock market. Everyone knew that Mama Liao's place was the finest.

"By 2005 I had branched out. I had the house near Zhongnanhai, and another connected to the leadership compound at Jade Spring Mountain, northwest of the city. In 2006, I was able to buy this place.

"But by then the attraction of Beidaihe was not just the sea air and the flowers. It was any air at all. It was being able to see the ocean. In Beijing you could barely see the end of the block. In Beijing, by 2005, no one went out without a face mask. All but the very poorest had ventilators, regular gas masks with filters and supplementary oxygen. You never saw anyone's face on the street. On a good day you could see half a mile. The rich never went outside at all. Houses and cars had their own special atmospheres.

"The most common causes of death were emphysema, asthma, and lung cancer. Almost everyone had them.

"And the water. The Chang Jiang—the Yangtze—and the Huang He (Yellow River) regularly caught fire, they were so polluted. The common people got sick all the time from the water. And even here, I can tell you, it was sometimes impossible to find rice that had not been grown in bad water, fruit that would not make you sick. The harbor just around the point here at Qinhuangdao turned black, actually black, like oil. Here at Beidaihe the waves washing up on the beach brought in scum, and sometimes sudsy foam, like a washing machine, but a meter deep or more. People could not swim, even here. You could not eat the fish caught here in the bay. The trees turned gray and yellow and started dying. All sorts of environmental diseases, cancers—my customers got more and more worried, especially about their children.

"And why was this? We had environmental laws. They were very strict. But no one had to obey them. It was just a matter of paying of the inspector. If anyone sued, you paid off the judge. Believe me, I heard it all in here, night after night. It's how people got by.

Everybody was on the take. I sometimes felt I ran the only honest establishment in Hebei.

"Crime was even worse. The cops were too busy taking money. It got so you just couldn't go on the street. Gangsters all had their own territory. You couldn't go through without paying—and sometimes they wanted more than money, especially if you were an attractive woman. I had to hire guards, trained men with guns. I never went anywhere except in my car. I bought an armored limousine in 2004. You had to have them. My driver was a large fellow with a degree in kung fu and a big automatic. I never let my girls go out without one of my guards right next to them.

"The older people started to talk about how wonderful it was when Mao was alive—can you believe it?—how the air was clean and you could walk the streets.

"It wasn't just publishing. Everything had its 'black' channel. They say half the economy, maybe more, was 'black'—stolen goods, kickbacks, illegal gambling, drugs.

"Drugs were the worst thing. They just flooded in after 1997, when the border with Hong Kong went down. They just got more and more popular. By 2005 my clients' children and grandchildren were getting addicted—not just a little marijuana, but amphetamines, cocaine, opium, heroin, and new 'designer drugs' like XMD12 and syndorphin.

"The word everyone used was *luan*—chaos. The economy slowed in 2002, and really fell apart in 2006. Between the pollution and the corruption, no one could really produce much.

"Energy was a real problem. We couldn't seem to get enough oil for our factories and transportation, and foreign companies kept jacking the price up or withholding the oil because they hadn't been paid on the last shipment, or they didn't trust our money—always some complaint.

"Foreign investment dried up. They were too scared. My customers used to bring me foreigners—American, French, British,

German. Not Japanese, I told them never bring me any Japanese. After what they did to my family and my country in the war, I could never allow them in my house. But the other foreigners— they would be working out some big deal, and throw in a night at Mama Liao's place to win them over, everybody have a good time together. After 2006 they stopped coming. In 2009, inflation got completely out of control. Money meant nothing. People's savings evaporated. I hardly ever went out. The streets were too scary, filled with angry crowds, homeless peasants camping on the sidewalks.

"And then came Hou Ju. I thank the gods every day for Hou Ju. I had met him, of course. Xi Dan, a member of the Military Affairs Commission, brought him here one night. He was a general, but of course there are hundreds of generals. A fine young man, handsome, yes, but very serious. Didn't go in the rooms with the girls. Just sat and talked—even with me. I liked that. Didn't drink much, a couple of beers.

"Next I heard of him was that fight with the Russian Far Eastern Republic. They had discovered that enormous oil field on the Amur outside of Khabarovsk—on land that used to be China's, land that we have always claimed. I tell you all these things because you look so young, and you are an American, you might not remember how Hou Ju came to be who he is.

"The government pressed its claim to the oil on the Amur, but the RFER reply was very rude, and in 2004 Hou Ju invaded. He took an army from the Shenyang military region over the border, had a quick battle at Ussuriysk, north of Vladivostok, beat them, and dictated terms. He was brilliant at strategy. The force he faced was much bigger than his own.

"He became a hero. He was the one beautiful thing in China, the one thing that made people proud. When he made speeches, and when we saw him on the television, he was so beautiful—he had this kind of strength we had not seen in our leaders since Mao.

"Already, that early, I heard the important people who came to my houses talking about him. He intrigued them, though not like the common people, you understand? They were not given to hero worship. No, they thought he might be useful. But they didn't know how to use him yet.

"He talked about two things. He talked about how the world could not keep China poor by keeping us from oil that was rightfully ours. And he talked about how we must clean up our society—the corruption, the pollution, the crime.

"And he kept doing things. After Ussuriysk, they had put him on the Military Affairs Commission, and he came up with the whole South China Sea campaign in 2007—they took every island in that sea, from the Paracels, and the Spratlys, and Mischief Reef, all the way down to the islands off of Indonesia, and every one had an oil field around it.

"He capped that in 2009, when he finally went for Taiwan. It was the invasion that no one in the world thought we could do. But he did it, a million men in 10,000 boats, a massive and very bloody battle that cut off Taipei—and then the terms were very generous, just like we gave Hong Kong.

"He was far more than a hero. People loved it. They were desperate for something to cheer for. And my customers—the entrepreneurs, the generals, the government ministers—they liked it, too, most of them. They thought, maybe he will save us. Maybe he can fix China. Many of them sent him messages of support. Some sent him money, invitations.

"Then one night, right in my living room just outside Zhongnanhai, I heard the conversation that changed history. About a dozen men—the Party chairman, several billionaires, including one that really represented the black economy, the smugglers and drug kings and all that, two generals from the Military Affairs Commission, several others—a group that altogether, you could say, ran China. They talked about Hou Ju, how he was capable of putting some spine back in the country. Even the black economy people liked the idea. There was far too much competition for their taste. And the men believed that they could control Hou Ju. So they decided. The next day government made him commander in chief, which they had never called anyone.

"As soon as they had done that, he went after Wuhan. The city had become the private reserve of a gangster named Hong Luo. Every kind of corruption flowed to him. He had some dispute with the local army commander, and he had his men ambush the garrison. Killed every last one.

"The government thought this was a very delicate situation. It opened a line of communication and announced it was negotiating with Hong. It ordered the Army to keep its distance.

"Well of course the Army adored Hou Ju, and when he told them to go into Wuhan, they went—two armored divisions. He had Hong's head displayed on a gold plate in a department store downtown. Then he went through the city, street by street, putting things in order. He replaced every judge with men who had the fear of Hou Ju in them. He put the fear into the local police, told them they had thirty days to round up all the criminals in town, or they'd be in prison, too. Suddenly Wuhan was a safe place. There were these huge public demonstrations down there. People were so happy.

"Now the big people were really split. Half said, 'Isn't this what we wanted him to do?' The other half thought he was out of control, very dangerous. The government, especially, and the top Party men. I know, they talked about it to me. They said, 'After all, he's the criminal, he went against orders.'

"So the government removed him as commander in chief, and ordered him back to Beijing to stand court martial. Big mistake. He got on the video conference system and asked the Thirty-eighth Army Group and the Fourth Army Group—they were stationed around Beijing—whether they were with him or the government. Did they want China to go on the way it had been going? Or did they want it like Wuhan?

"In the early morning—it happened to be June 4, 2010—the tanks rumbled into Beijing and took over Tiananmen Square, Zhongnanhai, the great Hall of the People. At dawn, Hou Ju appeared at the top of Tiananmen Gate and announced the founding of the Second People's Republic of China. The Communist Party would be replaced by the People's Party. He announced the end of all crime and corruption, and the beginning of a true rule of law. The square was filled with cheering people. I think it was the loudest sound I ever heard."

"What about your customers, the elites," asked the American, "the Party men, the *taizi*, the entrepreneurs, the generals, the government people?"

"Most of them were in the square that morning. Most of them sent congratulatory messages, or asked to see him and pay their respects. They were all over him. But few of them survived. After all, he knew them. And every one of them was corrupt. I suppose he could have just retired them. But he thought they were dangerous. He had them executed. Most of my customers—gone."

"So your business must have suffered terribly."

"Oh no. He knew me, had been here a number of times. All the officers that sided with him were customers. No, I served the new elite as I had served the old—and a lot more safely, I must say. He even assigned guards here, like the ones you checked in with when you came in."

"So, it has been twelve years," said the reporter. "How do you think it has worked, for China?"

"You can judge, perhaps, as well as I."

There was a long silence across the small table, over the teapot and the little tray filled with muffins.

"Please," said Mama Liao, "you can speak freely. There is no place more private than Mama Liao's."

The reporter cleared his throat. "Well, there were a number of show trials. Hundreds of executions. There was the Communist rebellion in Sichuan, which he put down with extraordinary brutality, wiping out entire villages. And freedom of speech and the press has disappeared once more from China. It is as I understand the Mao years were."

"You have to be tough to keep together as big a country as China," said the old woman. "Nobody has done it in any other way. There has been a lot of grumbling in other countries about the Freedom Through Labor camps, the quick trials, and what some liberals consider the lack of human rights, like the right to demonstrate against the government, or the right to spit on the sidewalk anytime you like, or the right to vandalize things and insult people. But don't people have a right to feel safe from hoodlums, I ask you? Today, a virgin carrying a sack of gold could walk alone anywhere in China, at any time of night, in perfect safety. We call it 'Cruel, but fair.' "

"It's true she would be perfectly safe," said the reporter, "unless she ran across some of Hou Ju's People's Guard. I have documented scores of cases from across China in which the People's Guard have raped, killed, extorted, and stolen with impunity."

"Even a great man cannot keep control of his troops all the time."

"Somehow I don't think it's an oversight problem. It looks more like a policy. Hou Ju is considered the world's richest man by far. It used to be that the reason the state enterprises did not make money was because they were subsidizing the rest of the economy. Now they subsidize Hou Ju. I have uncovered a pattern of payments from most of the major state enterprises—coal, gold mines, oil, electric power. They calculate their yearly profit. They send that amount into special 'locked accounts' reserved for Hou Ju's personal use. It shows up on the balance sheet as 'regularized annual expenses,' and the profit shows as zero."

"I don't know about that. I do know he cleaned up the country. Judges are honest now. They have to be, or they'll be executed."

"They are honest, unless Hou Ju wants a case decided a certain way."

"Of course," said Mama Liao. "They're not stupid."

"He cleaned up the streets using roving gangs of men—no uniforms—to kill or terrorize street prostitutes, homeless people, homosexuals, retarded people, anybody they thought spoiled the landscape."

"I have heard those rumors, too. Don't tell me you believe them. He uses only legal means. And look how he cleaned up the environment—just look at our beautiful bay and the forest."

"That's another curious pattern that I have uncovered," the reporter went on. "The country is remarkably cleaner than it was twelve years ago. Yet in every province there are a few businesses— big ones—that pollute with impunity, belching smoke into the skies, pouring acid into the rivers. I have interviewed people who claim that the answer is very simple: These businesses make the proper payment to Hou Ju himself, and they get put on a list that the authorities never touch.

"All those top people executed just after he took power—the Party leaders, the businessmen, the gangsters," he continued. "He simply took all their property for himself. I checked on a number of them. And he's still doing it. Apparently, according to people I have talked to, if someone amasses a great estate that he likes, he just takes it. If he sees a woman he wants, he takes her—it doesn't matter if it is someone's wife or daughter. If anyone makes trouble, they just disappear. I heard several specific allegations of women being kidnapped and forced to work in your houses, for the pleasure of the elite of the People's Party and the People's Guard, and of Hou Ju himself."

"People will say anything. A great man always accumulates enemies, people who want to see him destroyed. You have been collecting these stories for some time now? You have been very diligent, I see. You are not the type of reporter who is pleased just to report the government line."

"No. I am very careful."

Liao got up a little stiffly. The shadows were lengthening across the lawn outside. "Well, I must go now and make sure that everything is ready for the evening."

The American rose also. "Thank you for your time, Grandma Liao, and for your candor." He paused, considering, then asked, "Aren't you concerned about what I might write?"

She waved him off. "Oh, I never worry about interviewers. We have very good censors, the Internet, the satellite television, everything is very well-controlled. Do you know how Hou Ju got the foreign satellite broadcasters to pay attention to what he did not want broadcast into China?"

"No, Grandma. How?"

"He was negotiating with them, and they just wouldn't see it his way. So he shot one down. Shot down a broadcast satellite. Cost them over a billion dollars. They didn't know he could do that. He is a man who will get his way." She chuckled, clearly tickled by Hou Ju's special brand of cleverness. "But you are not the ordinary interviewer. You are far more diligent. That is, in fact, why I invited you here to Beidaihe, to the Hotel California. Do you know that song well?"

"Yes."

"The words? Do you remember the last line?"

He stared down at this little old woman, his lips moving slowly.

"Think hard," she said. "The last line."

He said it to himself in English first, then in Mandarin. " 'You can check out any time you like, but you can never leave.' "

"Ah yes, you do remember."

He looked over her head. Two guards had entered the pool area, their automatic rifles unslung. Other guards had appeared on the lawn outside.

He looked back at her. "Hou Ju can't just have me eliminated. Too many people know where I am."

She pursed her lips. "Oh, he does worry about that sort of thing a great deal. His reputation in the American newspapers is precious to him. Don't worry, he won't execute you. Not for some time. He will want to know, first, everyone you talked to. He will want to know that the information is accurate. You will resist. They will do things to you. It will take some time. Goodbye."

She turned and walked to the doors. The guards passed her. As she reached the door an officer came in, the captain of the guard. He looked over the scene, and said to her, "Well-handled. Hou Ju will be pleased."

She looked back into the room and sighed. "A pity. He's a rather nice-looking young man."

The captain laughed. "Oh, we'd be happy to give him to you when we are done."

"Hmmph. When you're done, he won't be nice-looking."

Part Three

Implications
What Does All This Mean?

Here at the end we draw implications from our scenarios. First we note the different roles we each play in relating to China: organizational, personal, civic, and parental. Second, we draw implications for six different issues coloring our relationship with China. Third, we conclude with a section on how to use these scenarios. The future of China has profound implications for each of us in our several roles.

Organizational   The future of China affects us in our organizational roles, as leaders and members of corporations, churches, nongovernmental organizations, unions, and philanthropic organizations. How should our organization engage with China? Should we treat China as the new Gold Rush, looking for ways to extract quick profits?

For nonprofits, the question is still there: Should we look for ways to extract quick conversions, score easy points, or get the most money from our contributors by hammering on the Chinese? Or should we look for ways to invest in a stable future, to build long-term relationships in China, even if that means forgoing the quick points, the easy work?

Do we have any leverage on the policies of China's leaders? If we do not have any leverage, or if our leverage is very small, should we stand by our beliefs anyway, no matter what the cost?

Or should we make our beliefs known and then engage with China anyway, just to be part of the process on the ground in the world's largest nation? What strategy will have the greatest benefits in the long run?

Personal   It affects us personally—in our career choices, our buying decisions, and greatly in what kind of world we live in, in whether that world feels safe, humane, and sustainable or threatening, brutal, and destroyed. Should I try to start a business in China? Should I buy Chinese goods? Should I join voluntary organizations that have an interest in China? Should I travel there? Should I try to help bridge the gap in my community between people of Chinese origin and others?

Civic   We have decisions to make as citizens. Shall we encourage our governments to open up more trade with China? Should our governments engage China on human rights issues? What is the most effective way to do that?

Parental   In many ways, the decisions are deepest for us when we look at China as parents. How China's history unfolds over the next few decades may say more than we imagine, more than any other single factor, about what kind of world our children will inherit.

Six Implications

Whichever role you find yourself playing, there are six implications that surface from these scenarios. First, as the range of our scenarios demonstrates, choices matter. The future is not predetermined. Second, Japan will play a major role in whatever scenario unfolds. Third, as the Chinese remind us, building relationships is of paramount importance. The last three implications touch on the sore spots in America's foreign relations policy toward China: constructive engagement or containment, Taiwan, and human rights.

One: Choices Matter

However we look at China, through lenses that sort for environmental concerns, business opportunities, strategic geopolitical and military aspects, or human rights issues, the uncertainties are huge. All of the scenarios that we have painted, and many others that you can imagine, could happen. They are plausible. The future of China is in no sense pre-determined. The choices that we make matter. Whether we are foreign policy-makers, offshore Chinese or mainland Chinese, Taiwanese or Japanese, entrepreneurs, corporate business-builders, or human rights advocates, our actions will make a difference. What will mold the future of China are not impersonal forces of nature, but human actors making choices. Consider, for instance, the difference between Brazil and Argentina as compared to Singapore, Hong Kong, and Japan over the last fifty years. Brazil and Argentina have major natural resources, big populations, and a lot of land. Japan has few natural resources, and Singapore and Hong Kong have none of which to speak. Japan has a large, densely packed population. Singapore and Hong Kong have small, densely packed populations. In 1945, Japan was horribly poor, devastated by war, disease, and famine. Hong Kong and Singapore were poor, rickety, sleepy, colonial backwaters. Hong Kong was soon overrun by more than a million refugees from the Communist victory. Today, Westerners see the Japanese, Singaporeans, and the Chinese of Hong Kong as industrious and quick to adapt. Fifty years ago, Westerners thought of them as lazy, disorganized, corrupt, and mired in tradition.

Look at the purchasing power per person (PPP), in equivalent U.S. dollars, of the world's top seven nations:

Luxembourg $31,090

United States $25,860

Kuwait $24,500

Switzerland $24,390

Hong Kong $23,080

Singapore $21,430

Japan $21,350

Where are resource-rich Argentina and Brazil? They are still struggling up from "developing nation" status, with PPP per capita of
$8,920 and $5,630, respectively. The difference lies not in resources,
or even in some mysterious national characteristic of industrious-
ness, but in the decisions the rulers and people of each country have
made—and the decisions by others that have affected them—over
those fifty years. Choices made well or poorly will determine how
China's future unfolds.

Two: The Single-largest Issue

If there is one overarching issue that has more potential than any
other to affect the future of China, it is whether the management of
the three-way relationship between the United States, Japan, and
China helps integrate China into the world system. It is imperative
that the United States and Japan, the two largest national economies
in the world, and China's two closest powerful neighbors in a geopolitical sense, have a strategy for managing that relationship. At the
moment, neither country displays a thoughtful, long-term, consistent strategy, let alone a coordinated, mutual strategy.

Three: Building Relationships

Any outsider who wants to participate in China must be realistic
about the time frame. No part of the process will be instantaneous.
Successful efforts take a long time. They organize for decades, building a base for the future, becoming not just a branch factory for the
home operation, but in many ways a Chinese company.

For the same reason, the blend of local Chinese, overseas
Chinese, and people of other nationalities is important. As the chief

executive of one major multinational put it, "You cannot develop in China with white faces." If you try, you and your management will be perpetual outsiders.

On the other hand, you also cannot develop in China with purely homegrown Chinese faces, or you will not be able to integrate the operation with the rest of your organization. Chinese accounting practices are generally opaque to outsiders, and Chinese management practices and methods of dealing with bureaucracy can be equally baffling. The cultural translation problems far outweigh the simple language problems. China is a relationship-based culture. It takes a long time to establish those relationships.

Four: The Self-fulfilling Prophecy

When we begin to understand how important China is in the future of the rest of the world, and how rapidly China is growing and changing, it becomes easier to picture China as a potential enemy, powerful and unpredictable. But here we come face to face with a big dilemma: The more the rest of the world thinks of China as a potential enemy, and acts on that fear, the more our fear creates a self-fulfilling prophecy. A China that other powers are attempting to "contain" is a China that feels itself increasingly in a trap from which it cannot escape without belligerent military action.

Right now the West, and particularly the United States, has a unique window of opportunity. Even if China continues to grow at a prodigious rate, the United States has ten to fifteen years during which it will remain materially stronger and more powerful. This is a time in which no great belligerent superpower is facing the United States on the world stage. Neither the United States nor China is at war with a client of the other country. They have no large national interests over which they are at loggerheads, and both have major mutual interest in growing trade and economic stability. China is not yet one of the major polluters of the world, not yet one of the major energy importers.

During this period the United States has a fair amount of maneuvering room and can afford the luxury of being generous. It is not a time to try to "contain" China, but a time to nurture that long-term working relationship, and then to establish some rules for engagement. For instance, since World War II, the United States has guaranteed freedom of passage for all nations through the Straits of Malacca—which has helped relieve Japan of any concern about access to Middle East oil. Similar assurances could relieve China of the need to station ships in the area in order to ensure its access to energy supplies.

In fifteen years, each one of these factors will be different. This is an opportunity too rare and important to miss.

Five: Taiwan

In this context, it becomes extremely important that the United States do everything possible to minimize the possibility that Taiwan will become a trigger for conflict.

Strategically, Taiwan carries for Chinese military planners much of the weight that Cuba did for the United States during the Cold War, as a giant, permanent aircraft carrier, barely a bow shot (in this age) offshore, moments away by missile, independent, highly militarized, and under the influence of foreign powers. Yet the analogy is not complete, for Taiwan has been a part of China for more than 300 years, since the Qing annexed it in 1683. Here an ounce of ambiguity is worth a pound of clarity. Announcing unequivocally that the United States would defend Taiwan if it were attacked could be destabilizing, strengthening the hard-line forces within the Beijing hierarchy, inflaming Chinese public opinion, and giving Beijing an excuse for flexing its military muscles. Such an announcement would put the United States at the mercy of any trigger-happy Chinese or Taiwanese military officer, and it could possibly drag the United States into a war that it did not want.

On the other hand, announcing unequivocally that the United States considered the Taiwan issue a purely internal affair and that it would do nothing to defend it would be equally destabilizing, forcing Taiwan into an even more frantic arms buildup and tempting China to strike as soon as possible.

Li Peng, Jiang Zemin, and other Beijing leaders have explicitly proposed the terms of Hong Kong's reversion as a model for the eventual reunification of Taiwan with China—and leaders on Taiwan immediately rejected the model. Yet the model is there in front of the eyes of Taiwan and the world. If China sticks to the letter and spirit of its agreements in Hong Kong, if Hong Kong truly is able to survive as a semiautonomous cultural, political, and economic entity under Beijing's wing, a peaceful return of Taiwan to the motherland becomes increasingly likely. But because Taiwan has an active democracy, it is even harder to predict what they as a society will vote to do.

Six: Human Rights

It is likely that when the United States and global organizations such as Amnesty International speak to the Chinese leadership about human rights, they are using the wrong language. The fundamental assumption of this dialogue—that individuals have inherent rights that all governments must respect—is not a shared assumption. It would be catastrophic to press the universalistic view that Western values favoring individuals over social cohesion are superior and should obviously be adopted by all intelligent people. The West can do great harm—and the biggest wrong the West could do would be to give China the sense that the West wishes to dominate them.

For its own political purposes, the United States has long been fully prepared to compromise its principles in favor of its interest, to tolerate the intolerance and harsh justice of some societies, such as Islamic Saudi Arabia, Taiwan under Chiang Kai-shek, or Iran under the Shah—as long as these regimes were clearly on our side in geopolitical struggles. This has not escaped the leadership in Beijing, who see a certain arbitrariness in the American desire to flail them with human rights demands.

There is a constructive dialogue to be had. There is also a great deal of work to be done, but it must be done in a language that makes sense in Beijing. The Party and government leadership have only one part of their roots in Leninist "statism." The other root is classically Chinese, even Confucian. There is nothing in Leninism, or in Confucianism or other classical Chinese models, about individual human rights. But there is a great deal in Confucianism about a government's responsibility for the sufferings of its citizens. And Chinese culture holds quite strongly to the idea of "face." When Beijing has responded positively to U.S. overtures on specific human rights issues, it has not been because they finally understood what the United States was saying about human rights. It has been because, at that particular moment, Beijing felt powerfully its need to build "face" in the West.

The overreaching values that the West must keep pressing for are openness and the rule of law. Gently, over time, in small ways, the West must press what China has to gain and what it has to lose.

How to Use
These Scenarios

How should you use this book to shape your strategy with respect to China? Part of the answer will depend on what industry you are in. Aerospace and apparel pose different strategic challenges. We will not try to tick off strategic implications of the scenarios industry by industry—it would be an endless task that would prove tedious to anyone who was *not* in aerospace or apparel or whatever. But we can describe a couple of ways that scenarios can help in framing strategy. The emphasis here is on process rather than content. There are some well-rehearsed methods for moving from scenarios to strategy.

The first approach moves from scenarios to strategic options; the second starts with an existing strategy and tests it against a range of scenarios. Either approach adds value. Let's start with the first approach, which divides into two branches. Then we will move on to the second approach.

Let's say that you have the germ of an idea, but you do not yet have a full-blown strategy. Let's say you would like to sell silk scarves. You have not yet gone into business. You do not have suppliers, you do not have distributors, and you have not yet developed a detailed strategy for building your business. Starting with just the germ of an idea, you read the three scenarios, then you pick one and imagine that it is more than just one scenario among several. Think of it as a predestined future. You have received a phone call from

God, or an expensive forecast from a high-priced consultant, and you have reason to believe that "China Web" is an accurate description of China's coming decades.

Now ask yourself: If "China Web" is the future, what implications does that forecast have for the silk scarf business? What are the challenges posed by "China Web?" For example, will there be many competitors in this high-growth future? But communication with your Chinese suppliers will be easy. And an open China will make exporting a cinch. As China leapfrogs the industrial revolution to join the information economy, environmental pollution should not retard growth, and so on.

The point is to think of yourself as a merchant of silk scarves within that imaginatively constructed future, and then think of all the actions you would want to take in order to thrive in that future. Come up with a list of eight to ten strategic options that make sense in just that scenario.

After you have gone through that exercise for one scenario, then repeat it for each of the other scenarios. Forget that each scenario is just one among others and treat it as fate, as destiny, as the sworn testimony of a genie who has emerged from Aladdin's lamp and can tell you all that you would ever want to know about China's future. Exercise your imagination as a silk scarf merchant in each of the several scenarios, and generate a list of strategic options appropriate to each scenario. Consider first the challenges, shortages, threats, and opportunities posed by each scenario—what we call the *implications* of that scenario. Then come up with ways to meet those challenges, make up for those shortages, defend against those threats, capitalize on those opportunities. These are your *strategic options*, a long list that is a precursor to a more focused strategy.

Once you have lists of strategic options for each of the scenarios, then you return to the present. Three scenarios are wonderful; three strategies are not. You need one strategy if you and your employees are to work together in a coherent and consistent way. So what do you do with three lists of strategic options?

There is a fork on this first path that leads with scenarios and the germ of an idea. Down one path lies what we like to call "a strategy for all seasons." Down the other, a strategy that fits just one scenario. The strategy for all seasons comes from considering all of the items on all of the lists and asking, "Which of these many strategic options could we start working on tomorrow without fear of failure in one or another scenario?"

Some options may show up on all of the lists. Call them the "no brainers." They make up the beginnings of a strategy for all seasons. They are robust across the range of scenarios. Next look for the "no painers," the options that look good in one or two scenarios and do not cause pain in the other scenarios. Finally, identify the "no gainers," those options that might look good in one scenario, but get you into trouble in the others. An obvious example of a "no gainer" would be an exit strategy that was appropriate to "The Thief of Beijing," but would leave money on the table in "China Web."

Once you have identified the no brainers and eliminated the no gainers, then it is worth prioritizing the no painers. If you are working with a team, give each person twenty poker chips (real or virtual) and ask everyone to allocate those priority chips using the following criteria: First, how well does a given option fit with the known strengths of your organization? Second, how much might you gain (or lose) in each scenario by implementing that option? This calculus need not be rigorously quantified on a first pass. All you are doing is getting a quick and fairly intuitive readout of the shared judgment of your entire team.

Once you tabulate the results of this prioritization of the no painers, and put the top scoring items together with the no brainers, you have the beginnings of a real strategy. You will have reaped the benefits of expanding your imagination for strategic options by projecting your thinking into several possible futures. And you will have wrestled with the uncertainty of not knowing which of those scenarios will actually unfold. By using the range of the scenarios to stimulate your imagination, then the prioritization exercise to narrow the several lists of options down to one short list, you will be well on the way towards a strategy for all seasons.

Once you have started from a set of scenarios to nurture the germ of an idea into a first pass at a strategy for all seasons, then you are ready for the second approach to using scenarios for strategy. You are ready to wind-tunnel your strategy through each of the scenarios. But before getting to that second approach, let's not forget the second path. Down that second path you branch away from a strategy for all seasons and settle instead on a strategy that optimizes for just one of the scenarios. In order to take this path, you need a set of early indicators that give you confidence in just one scenario.

What do we mean by "early indicators"? These are the little signs of the big changes that make up the scenario, not the events of the scenario itself. What are the earliest warning signals that suggest an incoming scenario? When looking for early indicators, you do not wait for the events that tell you that you are already in that scenario. You look for the precursors of those events, the buds before the bloom, the rains upstream that precede the floods downstream, or, even better, the weather forecasts that predict those rains upstream.

Early indicators for "China's Web" might include sales of pagers, cell phones, and modems. Early indicators for "New Mandarins" might include the career paths of the children of today's older leaders; or, to the contrary, the spread of democratic elections that would substitute democratically elected leaders for dynastic mandarins. Early indicators for "The Thief of Beijing" would include any signs of instability or disintegration of the rule of law. For each scenario, it is worth constructing a list of a dozen or so indicators that can be monitored on a regular basis. In addition, some early indicators may be anecdotal: one-off events, like the bombing of the Chinese embassy in Yugoslavia, that might tip the course of history toward one scenario or another.

When a combination of singular events, plus a preponderance of regularly monitored indicators, all begin to suggest that one scenario is emerging as much more probable than the others, then it is time to implement the strategic options appropriate to just that scenario. Even if it is a bad scenario, like "The Thief of Beijing," the good news is that you are not surprised. You are not caught off guard. You will not be blindsided by events because you will have already mentally rehearsed that future. You have a set of responses ready. You have a set of strategic options that were developed after careful deliberation during calmer moments when your back was not pressed against the wall by the force of unanticipated events.

Likewise for upside scenarios. If early indicators for "China's Web" start showing up in the news, if you have already thought through the steps you need to take in order to capitalize on the opportunities offered by "China's Web," if you have your line of credit, your suppliers in place, your distributors identified, then you can hit the ground running and take full advantage.

Of course, keep your ears and eyes open for signs of the other scenarios. What you do not want to do is pick one scenario and bet the farm. If you narrow your vision to just one scenario, then you lose whatever advantage scenario planning has to offer. You are back to the practice of traditional strategic planning based on a single forecast. So even if a preponderance of early indicators suggest that it is time to implement the strategic options appropriate to just one scenario, you remain sensitive to the signs of other scenarios. Try not to adopt a tunnel vision toward just one future.

So much for starting with scenarios in order to generate strategic options. We have considered two branches down that path: one branch led to a strategy for all seasons; the other, to a set of strategic options appropriate to the scenario most strongly suggested by leading indicators. Now what about the other path, the one that starts from an existing strategy? How then to use scenarios? Or how to use the scenarios still further when the first path has yielded a strategy.

Here the operative metaphor is that of a wind tunnel. The idea is to use the scenarios to "flight test" the strategy under different conditions. The set of scenarios now functions like a flight simulator. We can see how durable, how resilient, how robust is the strategy. How well does it behave under different conditions? How does it hold up under hard times? How well does it perform in good times?

Just as aerodynamic engineers use wind tunnels to test their designs and make improvements, so can scenarios help us to tweak our strategies so that they will perform better under real conditions. Just as flight simulators help to train pilots to respond appropriately to the different conditions they will meet in the air, so the use of scenarios can help to train executives to respond appropriately to the different business conditions represented by different scenarios.

Wind tunnels and flight simulators are fairly expensive pieces of equipment to build and program. But they are not as expensive as building real airplanes and crashing them into the ground. Likewise, developing and using scenarios demands a considerable investment of time and money, but the investment is well worth it if the reward is keeping your company from crashing into bankruptcy. Or, alternatively, the investment will repay itself many times over when your scenarios allow you to locate and optimize that updraft that others miss.

For Our Children

For each of us, a world of peace and prosperity is preferable to a world of conflict and hardship. The single-largest reason why we might end up with one or the other is the fate of China. If China becomes troubled, its pain will cause disruptions and dislocations all across the globe. This is not Rwanda or Bosnia, a sad and regrettable tragedy that can nonetheless be contained, that does not have to affect us. This is one-fifth of humanity. When we think about China, we must also think about our children. Creating room for China on the world stage is the best way to create a world in which our children do not have to go to war with theirs.

Index